6.50
57893

# The Redesigned Forest

Chris Maser

R. & E. Miles
San Pedro ✳ 1988

Copyright © 1988 by Chris Maser
All rights reserved.
Library of Congress Catalog Number: 88-092034
ISBN: 0-936810-16-5 (paperback)
    0-936810-17-3 (hardback)
Manufactured in the U.S.A.
91 90        5 4 3

The author would like to thank the following authors and publishers for being so generous with their permissions:

Fritjof Capra, *The Tao of Physics*, Copyright © 1975, 1983. Reprinted by arrangement with Shambhala Publications, Inc., 300 Massachusetts Ave., Boston, MA 02155.

Vernon Gill Carter and Tom Dale, *Topsoil and Civilization*, Revised edition. Copyright © 1955, 1974 by the University of Oklahoma Press.

Portions Reprinted by Permission from *A Course in Miracles*. Copyright © 1975, Foundation for Inner Peace, Inc.

Hermann Hesse, *Siddartha*. Copyright © 1951 by New Directions Publishing Corp. By permission.

C. G. Jung, *The Undiscovered Self*, Copyright © 1957, 1958. By permission of Little, Brown and Co.

Patterson, Lewis and Sheldon Fisenberg, *The Counseling Process*, Third Copyright © 1983 by Houghton Mifflin Co. Used with permission.

E. A. Pessemier, *Product Management, Strategy and Organization*, 2nd edition. Copyright © 1982, John Wiley & Sons, Inc., by permission.

Dr. Seuss, *The Lorax*. Copyright © 1971 by Dr. Seuss and A. S. Geisel. Reprinted by permission of Random House, Inc.

Printed on recycled and acid-free paper.

R. & E. Miles
Post Office Box 1916
San Pedro, California 90733
(213) 833-8856

To Zane

my wife and learning partner
I dedicate this book
with love, respect and gratitude.
You are my constant challenge
to grow, to change, to become. . . .

# TABLE OF CONTENTS

# PREFACE

The pace of life was slow with few formal laws governing human behavior when North America was settled. And the seemingly limitless quantity and quality of resources favored the staunch individualism with which the nation was forged.

Times have changed. We are now a society, based on historical abundance, struggling to learn how to manage limited resources. We are experiencing the dualities of adolescence in that we want both the irresponsibility of youth and the privileges of adulthood. We still want a boundless supply of high-quality products, but we can no longer maximize both quantity and quality simultaneously; past abundance has become present limitations and, if we are not careful, future scarcity. Even as I write, we are fighting over who is going to get the last of the limited resources rather than striving to ensure their existence for the future.

With the passing of each decade—and a world population that reached five billion people in 1987 and will grow three billion more individuals in the next 35 years—our society becomes increasingly complex and confused. We seem mesmerized by numerical units (identification numbers) and commodities, our attention riveted on managing the world for products while we lose sight of human dignity. Tragically, it is this neglected area—human dignity—that is the barometer of our well-being. The wholeness, the inner state of self-worthiness of each member of society, is the individual mirror image of society's value system. When that value system faithfully reflects the individual's needs for wholeness, then society and its components are in harmony. The paradox is that managing products is a numbers game, whereas human dignity, which is based on spirituality, intuition, creativity, imagination, dreams, and experiences, is not quantifiable.

Inherent in a world of rapidly growing population and limited resources is the increase in formal laws that stifle human expression and threaten human dignity. How? Competition becomes severe, the pace of life quickens, leading to frustration that often manifests itself in cynicism. A cynic is a fault-finding critic who believes that human conduct is motivated solely by self-interest and therefore has little or no faith in people. Cynicism is a charge that is often leveled at selected individuals or groups. Inherent in the choice of whether or not to be cynical, however, is the question of having the courage to accept responsibility for one's actions. A cynic, by definition, projects blame to others.

Another tendency of human beings faced with frustration is to defend a point of view, which is synonymous with individual survival. There are as many points of view as there are people, and everyone is right from his or her vantage point. There can be no solution, however, when each person remains committed to defending his or her narrow interest. The alternative is to define an environmental issue and focus on it. If a crisis is defined as an issue, which is a question to be answered, both positive and negative options become apparent and winning or losing environmentally becomes a choice.

To the Chinese, crisis means "dangerous opportunity." Crisis is defined as: The decisive moment (as in a literary plot); an unstable or crucial time or state of affairs whose outcome will make a decisive difference for better or worse. Juncture, a crossroad, is a synonym for crisis. Every crisis has two options—positive and negative. In field and forest ecology, Nature makes the choices. In human society, the choice is ours. That we tend to avoid change, to hug our comfort zone, does not diminish the positive option, it only means that we have chosen to argue for our limitations instead of our potential, which always involves an element of risk.

Although individualism is good, even necessary, in the embryonic stages of an endeavor, it must blend into teamwork in times of environmental crisis. The setting aside of egos and points of view is necessary for teamwork because unyielding individualism prevents cooperation, resolution of issues, and achievement of goals. Teamwork demands the utmost personal discipline, which is the common denominator for success in any endeavor.

Even if we exercise personal discipline in dealing with current environmental problems, most of us have become so far removed from the land that sustains us that we can no longer see it as the embodiment of a continual process. Attention is focused instead on a chosen product, the success or endpoint of management efforts, and anything diverted to a different product is considered a failure.

It is a critical time to re-evaluate our philosophical foundation and to re-emphasize human dignity in management decisions. With a renewed focus on human dignity as a "product" of the resource decision-making process, we can broaden the philosophical basis of management to include forests and grasslands, oceans and societies rather than only a few selected commodities that they produce. Emphasis on human dignity in management will help foster teamwork that, in turn, nurtures mutual trust and respect rather that the "us against them" syndrome. The "us against them" syndrome exists because our dreams are too small; they are limited only to our own interests and therefore appear separate and in conflict. For example, I want old-growth trees, *or* I want woodfiber, *or* I want wilderness, *or* I want native trout, *or* I want clean water, *or, or.* . . . What we need instead is a collective dream large enough to encompass and transcend all our small, individual dreams in a way that gives them meaning and unity. If we dare to dream boldly enough, our special interests will both create and nurture the whole—a healed, healthy, sustainable forest that includes old-growth trees, *and* woodfiber, *and* wilderness, *and* native trout, *and* clean water, *and, and.* . . .

Now, more than ever, we must recognize that we are part of the human family and trust and respect each other as if human dignity truly were the philosophical cornerstone of society. We must also recognize and accept that we have one ecosystem that simultaneously produces a multitude of products. And we, as individuals and generations, as societies and nations, are both inseparable products of and tenants of that system, custodians for those who follow.

# ACKNOWLEDGMENTS

No book is the endeavor of a single individual; no book is a definitive treatise. Every book is a progress report written by committee. Although my name is on this book as the author, I have had several "co-authors" who have reviewed and commented on the entire manuscript. They are: Jo Alexander (Managing Editor, Oregon State University Press, Corvallis), Ronald O. Clarke (Department of Religious Studies, Oregon State University, Corvallis), Helen Engle (Board of Directors, Audubon Society, Tacoma, WA), Robert Hoffman (Biological Research Associate, Marine Science Center, Oregon State University, Corvallis), Robin Jacqua (Jungian Analyst, Eugene, OR), William H. Moir (Regional Ecologist, Region 3, USDA Forest Service, Albuquerque, NM), David Rittersbacker (Supervisor, Ochoco National Forest, USDA Forest Service, Prineville, OR), and Kris Wilder (Department of Horticulture, Oregon State University, Corvallis).

Sheila Till (Corvallis, OR) not only read and reread almost the entire manuscript but also patiently typed and retyped the early drafts.

Every project I have done that has turned out well has, at some point, found a champion to give it that final step towards excellence that I failed to see was missing. This book is no exception. Jean Matthews (Science Editor for the National Park Service) came forward to give whole-heartedly of her extremely sharp editor's eye and gentle touch. She took some of my rough sentences and made them smooth; she added clarity where there was fuzziness; and she added a perspective of long editorial experience where it was needed. Thus, in a very real sense, this book was written with Jean's help because she spent many hours, pencil in hand, helping me strive for that always challenging, often nebulous goal called excellence.

Each person named in these acknowledgments has added his or

her unique gift to the completion of this book. Thank you. And a final "Thank you" to the seemingly countless audiences who have patiently listened over the years while I "thought out loud." I am particularly grateful to those individuals from the audiences who have openly challenged the ideas and the way I expressed them, for you have caused me to constantly re-examine what I feel, what I think, what I say, and how I say it.

# INTRODUCTION

The *Corvallis Gazette-Times,* Corvallis, Oregon, 14 November 1986, carried the story "Changing a forest's character." The story opened: "Managers of the Siuslaw National Forest are introducing a plan today to gradually change the complexion [character] of the Coast Range forest. . . ." What does it mean to "change a forest's character?" Are character and appearance synonymous? Are character and forest products synonymous? Are character and forest processes synonymous? Character is defined as a conventionalized graphic device placed on an object as an indication of ownership, origin, or relationship. In the case of our forests, this means logging roads, single-species monocultures, genetically altered trees, etc. Thus, by definition, we are redesigning our forests from Nature's blueprint to humanity's blueprint. What does it mean to redesign the forest?

To better discuss the redesigned forest, I have divided this book into four parts. The differences between Nature's design of a forest and our design of a forest is examined in Part One. Why we insist on our design is examined in Part Two. Why we are afraid of change is examined in Part Three, and ways to integrate Nature's design with our design in an attempt to achieve sustainable forestry is examined in Part Four. Of necessity, there is overlap within and between the parts of this book. Although I have focused on the Pacific Northwest, the principles and concepts are generally applicable to all redesigned forests. Thus, it is critical that we both understand and accept the effects we cause by redesigning global forests, because we are simultaneously redesigning the structural and functional processes of the world, such as cycles in soil fertility, cycles in quality, quantity, and belowground storage of water, and cycles in climate. At risk is human survival on earth and in the universe. If we disarm the world of all weapons of war and continue to pollute and kill the global ecosystem that sustains us, our survival becomes only a matter of time. If we escape to another planet and do not change our thinking, the cause of global pollution, the only question for humanity again is time. We take ourselves with us wherever we go.

This book, gentle reader, is intended as a gift of ideas, and because a gift is free without strings or conditions, I have no expectations of you. I can't convince anyone of anything, so I'm not even going to try. If you find something of value between these covers, you may extract it and use it; if not, that too is okay.

I have written this book for four reasons. The first is to examine, as best I am able, what we are doing today in the name of "forestry," why we are doing it, and where our current management practices seem to be taking us. I have used numerous quotes to illustrate some of the points and to show the pervasiveness of some thought processes in our Western culture.

The second reason is simply to point out that we must have a sustainable forest before we can have a sustainable yield of forest products—any forest products: clean air, quality water, fertile soils, woodfiber, or spotted owls. I see no sustainable forests as I look around the world because humanity is summarily cutting them down and, where possible, replacing forests with fast-growing tree plantations. Although liquidation of the world's forests in favor of fast-growing tree plantations to maximize quick profits seems rational enough in the short term, as Solo (1974) indicates, it may not be so rational in the long term: "Throughout . . . [our] habitat on earth, . . . [our] technologies have been formed on the *assumption* [emphasis mine] that the autonomous system that produces the environment needed for life cannot be reached by what we do nor destroyed by us. And here, I think, a crucial change has come. The life system itself is no longer beyond the reach of . . . [our] technology nor beyond . . . [our] power to disarrange, degrade, and destroy. *This is a danger no age has ever faced before* [emphasis mine]."

The third reason is to show another part of us, the part we seldom see when we look into society's mirror. That view, so carefully hidden from ourselves, is our ability to love, trust, respect, and nurture both one another and the land. To have sustainable forests, for example, we must change our thinking; and to change our thinking, we must transcend our own special interests and encompass all interests in the forest as a whole. Such change will cast a lighter, cleaner image in society's mirror.

xviii

And the fourth reason I've written this book is to propose a new paradigm for forestry. Each new paradigm is built on a shift of insight, a quantum leap of intuition with only a modicum of hard, scientific data. But those clinging to the old paradigm demand irrefutable, scientific proof that change is needed. Such proof, of course, is not initially there in an ever-changing universe. The irony is that the old paradigm also began as the new, and also was challenged to prove change was necessary or even desirable. Time and human effort have proven the old paradigm to have been more right than its predecessor but still only partially right. So it is with the new paradigm: it too is more right than the old and eventually will be proven to be only partially right and in need of change.

After 20 years as a research scientist, I know that a paradigm, any paradigm, that has become comfortable has also become self-limiting. New data will not and cannot fit into the old paradigm because each paradigm is a carefully constructed impervious, rigid membrane of tradition that, like concrete, hardens with age and must periodically be broken, like the exoskeleton of an insect, if a new thought-form is to grow, a new vision is to move society forward. This is incredibly difficult for those whose total belief system and personal identity is invested in the old paradigm (Hopwood et al. 1988, Jablanczy 1988). And those of us who subscribe to the new paradigm, whatever it may be, must understand and accept that a new paradigm can survive only because it is supported on the shoulders of preceding paradigms, all of which were at one time new, young, and daring. There have been no failures on the part of those who adhere to the old paradigm, only changes that may have left them behind (Hyatt and Gottlieb 1987). And we who would replace the old paradigm must be wise enough to carry forward into the new that of value from the old. The day will come when our "new" paradigm also must perish of old age. May we therefore be merciful with those who cling to opposing views and remember that in their time they were right and on the cutting-edge.

Three things I would like you to understand before you read this book. First, I recognize, as we strive to maintain sustainable forests, that we are faced with the constant struggle of accepting change and its accompanying uncertainties and this often gives rise to fear of the future. We must therefore be gentle with one another and do whatever we do with love because there are no "enemies" "out there," only frightened people. Second, ideas change the world;

people change ideas. And people must change before ideas will change. Third, all we have in the world as human beings is each other; if we lose sight of each other, we have nothing.

## Part One

## NATURE'S DESIGN OF A FOREST
## VERSUS OUR DESIGN OF A FOREST

*You can't condemn that which you understand.*
—Goethe

"In a very real sense . . . the land . . . bears a record of what men write on it. In a larger sense a nation writes its record on the land, and a civilization writes its record on the land. . . ." (Lowdermilk 1975). Aldo Leopold (1966, p. 68) approached the same concept when he wrote:

> I have read many definitions of what is a conservationist, and written not a few myself, but I suspect that the best one is written not with a pen, but with an axe. It is a matter of what a man thinks about while chopping, or while deciding what to chop. A conservationist is one who is humbly aware that with each stroke he is writing his signature on the face of his land. Signatures of course differ, whether written with axe or pen, and this is as it should be.

A few years ago, while flying home from a month's detail in the Interior Department, in Washington, D.C., I came to the conclusion that the old adage, "Deeds speak louder than words" is true so far as it goes. What is left unsaid is that "motives speak louder than deeds." Motives determine what we look at and how we look at it. Our motives determine why and how we redesign Nature's forests; they also determine our willingness to understand, accept, and take responsibility for the effects our actions cause through time. Our motives therefore dictate the record our actions inscribe on the land.

In the course of examining our attempts to "improve" Nature's design, we will be fortunate indeed if we come to understand that Nature functions perfectly (Lee et al. 1986). Our perception of how Nature functions is imperfect.

*Nature designed a forest as an experiment in
unpredictability.
We are trying to design a regulated forest.*

In the summer of 1486, a few years before Columbus' epic
voyage, a fire swept through a watershed in the northern Coast
Range of Oregon and killed most of the existing forest on the east
side of a large stream. The fire was stopped by the stream. The old-
growth Douglas-fir forest survived on the west side of the stream,
and seeds from these trees were blown across the stream into the
burnt area during an early winter storm.[1] Most seeds were eaten by
small animals, but some remained to germinate. Of those that germinated, only a few survived the centuries.

When the stand was 350 years old, in 1836, a severe windstorm
blew over several of the trees, and some of them hit other trees on
their way down. One tree was hit hard enough that the protective
bark was removed near its base; the wound was only 6 inches wide
and 12 inches long. Although small compared to the size of the tree,
the wound attracted woodboring beetles that chewed their way into
the wounded area. In so doing, the beetles opened the wood to
spores of fungi that began to attack the tree's tissues. The fungus
spread, decomposing the tissues and weakening the tree over the
next century and a half.

By the time it was 425 years old, the tree had a large weakened
area 10 feet above the ground, and that year—1911—a newly
formed queen carpenter ant set up housekeeping in the area of the
old wound. The ant colony grew, and new tunnels were continuously chewed in the sapwood by worker ants intent on expan-
sion of the colony. A pileated woodpecker (Photo 1) found the ant
colony in 1970, and pecked a large, squarish hole into the main-
stream of ant life, where it returned periodically over the years to
dine on the ants.

In 1986, a windstorm, with gusts reaching 70 miles per hour, blew
over a small group of Douglas-fir trees that had been weakened by a
root rot fungus. One fell against the ants' tree, now 500 years old. It
broke off in the area of the old wound, and fell diagonally upstream

---

1. Scientific names are in Appendix 1

4

Photo 1. The pileated woodpecker, the largest woodpecker in the Pacific Northwest, feeds largely on carpenter ants that chew their colonial tunnels in dead wood.
(USDA Forest Service photograph by Evelyn L. Bull.)

into the water. There it rests until 1996, and creates habitat for fish and other organisms.

The tree moves gently up and down in place as winter storms and high water come and go. Then, in the year 2000, a warm chinook wind coincides with a 15-foot accumulation of wet snow above 4,000 feet elevation. Warm rains, accompanying the sudden melting of snow, swell the stream and flush the fallen tree into the river. It comes to rest on a gravel bar, where it lies for the next 15 years, until 2015. During those years, the tree traps silt carried by winter floods that, in turn, allows a thicket of alder trees to become established on the protected down-stream side of the fallen tree.

The winter of 2015 is heralded by a series of violent rainstorms, causing severe flooding that sweeps the tree downriver and out to sea. Heavy seas and strong winds move the tree northward several miles and cast it onto a beach. Barkless and battered it lies bleaching in the sun; still visible, however, are the holes made by the pileated woodpecker 45 years earlier (Photo 2).

A winter storm in 2100 again washes the tree out to sea, where it floats for a year and a half before it is seen by a 25-year-old tuna fisherman. Setting his nets, he makes a bumper catch under the floating tree, the only shade-producing structure for hundreds of miles in the open ocean.

In the winter of 2103, the tree is again carried toward land, and this time is deposited in a mudflat along an estuary. A storm in 2110 moves the now water-logged tree toward the mouth of the estuary where it finally sinks. Marine, woodboring invertebrates, such as gribbles, are attracted to the tree and penetrate its wood. The sunken tree is fragmented over the years as the marine invertebrates tunnel their way throughout it. In addition to fragmentation, much of the woodfiber is excreted in the feces of gribbles and other organisms that live in the wood. During this time, it has served as cover and habitat for gribbles, shrimp, crabs, and fish.

A series of violent rainstorms in 2190 causes severe flooding and the sunken tree begins to break into chunks that wash back and forth with the tides. By 2250, all that remains of the tree is the substance of its cells called lignin, which is now part of the organic material that enriches the floor of the continental shelf off the Pacific Northwest coast.

If one event in our story were changed, the whole history of events would be different. For example, if a mouse had chosen to

Photo 2. A drifted tree awash on a beach from a distant forest and time. The large holes are still evident where a pileated woodpecker excavated carpenter ants while the tree was still in the forest. (Photograph by author.)

eat that particular seed, the fisherman would not have made his bumper catch of tuna 764 years later. If, on the other hand, the tree had not been wounded in 1836, it might have been logged in 1950. The tuna fisherman would not have had his bumper catch, but instead he could have been born in a house made from the lumber of the tree cut 225 years earlier. Let's change just one more event. If the tree that fell in 1986 had hit the ants' tree at a different angle, it would not have fallen into the stream. It would therefore have decomposed on land and been recycled through bacteria, fungi, beetles, and myriad other pathways into the changing forest over the next 200 to 300 years (2186 to 2286). Again, since the tree would not have fallen into the stream, the tuna fisherman would have missed an excellent catch on that particular day in 2102. These are only three of the countless things that might have happened to change the entire course of events.

To predict means to foretell, and to foretell we must be able to foresee. Nature's design, however, is a continual flow of cause-and-effect relationships that precisely fit into each other and are constantly changing in space and time (Fig. 1).

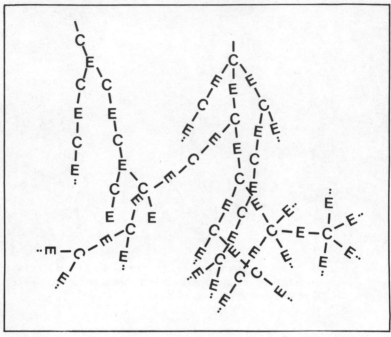

Fig. 1. Each cause has an effect, and each effect is the cause of another effect, *ad infinitum.*

The preceding story was about Nature's forest; what about our forest—the one we are trying to regulate? Regulate is defined as: to govern or direct according to rule; to bring under control of law or constituted authority; to bring order, method, or uniformity. What does it mean to design a regulated forest? Who has the authority to dictate how the forest will function? When we make decisions, how can we regulate events that we do not even know are coming, such as an ice storm that breaks trees, a volcanic eruption, a lightning strike or a spark from logging machinery that causes a fire? How can we regulate what will happen in 1, 10, 100, 500, or 1,000 years? We have seen what can happen by changing a single event in our story. What makes us think we know enough to dare to alter the entire dynamics of Nature's design over whole landscapes for all time when we cannot even predict what will happen from one year to the next? Hugh Prather (1980, p.73) put it nicely:

> We can't make the world work. There is no way to use it. We believe that if we could only change [regulate] this one thing within the situation, it would serve us well. But that assumes all things will remain equal. The situation cannot stay the same while one thing within it changes, because its very meaning depends on the contrast of dissimilar things. So after we succeed in changing "this one thing," there will arise something new in the situation that needs fixing, and on and on without rest.

Or as John Muir put it, "When you try to change any single thing, you find it hitched to everything else in the universe."

*Nature designed a forest of long-term trends. We are trying to design a forest of short-term absolutes.*

Trend is defined as a line of general direction or movement. In Nature's forest, a trend is defined by a multitude of interacting factors; these include:
1. location of event—on land, in water, in air, in the tropics, at the North or South Pole, in a valley . . .
2. size of event—inside the tip of a tree root, on an acre, over a landscape, over a continent . . .
3. duration of event— 10 seconds, an hour, a year, a century, a geological epoch . . .
4. time of event—day, night, season, year . . .
5. frequency of occurrence—hourly, daily, seasonally, annually . . .
6. distance between events—an inch, a foot, a yard, a mile, 1000 miles, 10,000 miles . . .
7. uniformity of event—uniform, roughly connected, disjunct . . .
8. type of event—physical, biological, combination . . .

The infinite variety of interactions among the above-listed factors creates an infinite variety of short-term trends that in turn are superimposed on a longer-term trend (Fig. 2-A), that is superimposed on

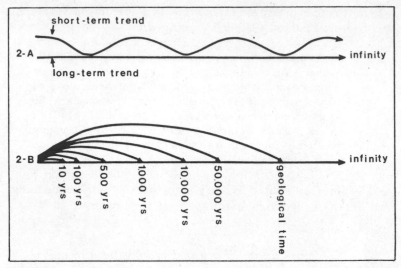

Fig. 2. Longer-term trends are composed of interrelated, dynamic, shorter-term trends.

a longer-term trend, ad infinitum (Fig. 2-B). By studying short-term trends (those we can comprehend) and projecting them over time, we can have, by definition of trend, some degree of predictability of Nature's actions.

There are two cautions. First, we must accept that all natural trends are neutral; the shorter the trend the more imperative is our acceptance of Nature's neutrality. Nature is always neutral. We as humans, however, never have a neutral thought; we therefore assign values to Nature's actions that are based on our perceptions of "good" and "bad." In so doing, we intromit into Nature's design an *artificial variable* that clouds our vision. We have robbed ourselves of our ability to predict the future by rejecting Nature's neutrality.

Second, we must view short-term trends in relation to long-term trends and long-term trends in relation to even longer-term trends. The more we telescope the present into the future, the more we will understand the present. The more we telescope the present into the past, the more we will understand the present. A knowledge of the past tells us what the present is built on and what the future may be projected on, but this is true only if we accept past and present as a cumulative collection of our understanding of a few finite points along an infinite continuum—the trend of the future.

10

Gentle reader, I suggest you fasten your seat belt for what only at first appears to be a "side trip." On this journey, however, there are no side trips any more than in worldly terms there are side effects; there are only direct causes and effects. And because wholeness demands largeness of grasp, we embark on a quick backward sweep of the events that led us to our present, dominant world view.

Although Nature gave us a degree of predictability over time— the ability to recognize and read the trend, we remain stubbornly committed to the concept of an absolute. The concept of an absolute probably arose in response to human fear of the unknown— observed natural forces (Fisher et al. 1986). This fear gave rise to religious ideas conceived in "the necessity of defending oneself against the crushingly superior force of nature" (Freud 1961, p. 21). In the sixth century B.C., the roots of Western science arose in the first period of Greek philosophy, a culture where science, philosophy, and religion were united. A split in this unity began with the assumption of a Divine Principle that stands above all gods and men. Thus began a trend of thought that ultimately led to the separation of spirit and matter and to the dualism that characterizes Western philosophy. Because the Christian church supported Aristotle's view that questions concerning the human soul and God's perfection took precedence over investigations of the material world (Capra 1975), Western science did not develop further until the Renaissance. Sir Francis Bacon then, in the late 1500's, gave humanity the ability to experiment when he defined what we call the scientific method. "Look," he told the world, "there is tomorrow. Take it with charity lest it destroy you" (Eiseley 1973).

Separation of rational and intuitive knowledge began with the ancient Greeks. Western philosophy embraced rational knowledge, that which is derived from our experience with objects and events in our immediate environment. Rational knowledge belongs to that realm of the intellect that discriminates, divides, compares, measures, and categorizes. It creates a world of distinctions whose opposites can only exist in relation to each other (Capra 1975). Capra (1975, pp. 27 and 28) put it this way:

> Abstraction is a crucial feature of this knowledge, because in order to compare and to classify the immense variety of shapes, structures and phenomena around us we cannot take all their features into account, but have to select a few significant ones. Thus

11

we construct an intellectual map of reality in which things are reduced to their general outlines. Rational knowledge is thus a system of abstract concepts and symbols, characterized by the linear, sequential structure which is typical of our thinking and speaking. . . .

The natural world, on the other hand, is one of infinite varieties and complexities, a multidimensional world which contains no straight lines or completely regular shapes, where things do not happen in sequences, but all together, a world where—as modern physics tells us—even empty space is curved. It is clear that our abstract system of conceptual thinking can never describe or understand this reality completely. In thinking about the world, we are faced with the same kind of problem as the cartographer who tries to cover the curved face of the Earth with a sequence of plane maps. We can only expect an approximate representation of reality from such a procedure, and all rational knowledge is therefore necessarily limited.

We in Western culture have become so linear in our thinking and so rational in our knowledge that we have forgotten that everything is defined by its relationship to everything else (Fig. 3).

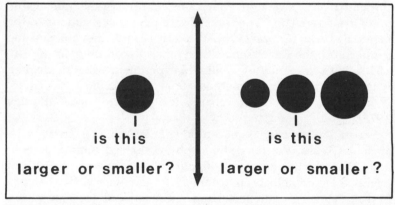

Fig. 3. Everything we visualize is defined by its relationship to everything else.

Nothing in our world can exist by itself; it can only exist in relation to something else. An example is our thinking in harvesting trees: that each stand is isolated from every other stand once we delineate the sale boundary. We divide and isolate and end up "managing" a linear sequence of special cases—stands of timber that are isolated in time and space only in our minds but nowhere in the landscape.

This point was clearly made while I was on the witness stand in federal court recently. At issue were two sales of old-growth timber. The assertion was repeatedly made that these were "just two sales" and would not have an impact on the remaining old-growth forest of which there was "ample." *Yet the fact is that we do not know how much old-growth forest exists, where it is, or how it is distributed over the landscape.* We do not know how one stand (that we delineate) relates to the rest of the old-growth forest or how the rest of the old-growth forest relates to any particular stand. How can we begin to understand the significance of the remaining old-growth forest until we relate the delineated units to each other in a local area, to the remaining old-growth forest on a watershed, to the remaining old-growth forest across a landscape? We see a timber sale as a numerically defined, commercial absolute, and in so doing, we fail to see its relation to the forest.

We have progressed little in understanding our relation to Nature. We still see Her as something to conquer and control. Our fear of Nature causes us to select a single, isolated point (a stand of old-growth trees) on the continuum of change, draw an illusionary line around it, quantify the volume of woodfiber, and define it as an unchanging absolute entity in time and space. An unchanging absolute and a dynamic relationship are diametrically opposed and mutually exclusive. *Nature deals only with trends—not absolutes.* A forest may therefore be summed up as a continuum of causes and effects that appear random in the short-term and patterned in the long-term. We thus forfeit our understanding and any predictability of the trends Nature has provided so long as we blindly commit ourselves to dealing in terms of artificial absolutes (Fig. 4).

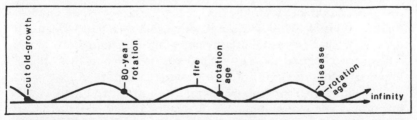

Fig. 4. Dynamic, short-term trend superimposed on a dynamic, long-term trend, with a false absolute (rotation age) fixed in time and space. As you can see, there is no guarantee that rotation age will be reached, despite all our planning.

13

*Nature designed a forest with diversity.*
*We are designing a forest with simplistic uniformity.*

Diversity is defined as having or being capable of having a variety of forms or qualities, of being composed of unlike or distinct elements. Stability is defined as the strength to stand or endure, the property that causes an entity to develop forces (processes) that restore the original condition when disturbed from a condition of equilibrium or steady motion. It follows that to some point diversity underlies stability; conversely, stability is built on diversity. Four questions lead to examples that demonstrate this point:

1. What happens when you remove just one part? While I was working in Nepal some years ago, a helicopter crashed and killed two people. As you might expect, a helicopter has a great variety of pieces that range from the large rotor, which whirls above the aircraft and keeps it flying, to a tiny screw that fastens the instrument panel to the cockpit. The particular problem in Nepal was with the engine. The engine is held together by many nuts and bolts. Each nut and bolt has a small sidewise hole through it so that a tiny "safety wire" can be inserted and the ends twisted together to prevent the tremendous vibration created by a running engine from loosening and working the nut off the bolt. The helicopter crashed because a mechanic forgot to replace one tiny safety wire that kept the lateral control assembly together. A nut vibrated off its bolt; the helicopter lost its stability, and the pilot lost control. All this was caused by one missing piece of diversity that altered the entire functional dynamics of the aircraft. The helicopter's engine had been "simplified" by one piece—a small length of wire. Which was the most important part in the helicopter, the large, visible rotor or the tiny, invisible wire? The point here is that each part (structural diversity) has a corresponding relationship (functional diversity) with every other part and they can provide stability only by working together within the limits of their designed purpose.

2. What happens when you "simplify" a process? I am elected mayor of a city whose budget is overspent, I guarantee that I can balance the budget. All I have to do, in a simplistic sense, is remove some services whose total budgets add up to the overexpenditure. I said in a "simplistic sense" because it is not that simple. What would happen, for example, if I removed all police and fire services?

Would it make a difference—if the price were the same and the budget could be balanced—if I removed garbage collection instead?

The trouble with such a simplistic view is that I am looking only at the cost, not at the *function* performed by the service that I propose to eliminate. I am simplifying the city's diversity by removing one or two pieces—service(s)—without paying attention to the functions performed by those services. To remove a piece of the whole—in this case a city service—may be acceptable provided we know which piece we are removing, what it does, and what effect the loss of its function will have on the stability of the system as a whole.

3. What happens when you "mine" so-called renewable resources? Since mining is an entirely different function from farming, we need to make another short hop back into history to see how we made this unlikely connection. The European farmers of early North America, with their small, diversified family farms, provided increased structural diversity, and therefore increased habitat diversity through a good mix of food, cover, and water. The many small, irregular fields with a variety of crops created an abundance of structurally diverse edges, and tillage offered a variety of soil textures for burrowing animals. Uncultivated fence-rows and ditch banks provided strips that not only acted as primary habitat for some species but also provided travel lanes between fields for other species. But all this resulted in "small crop yields because of competition from other plants and because insects, birds, and mammals all took their share of the crop" (Pimentel 1971, p. 212).

In modern agricultural practice in North America, however, large fields often are planted with a single species, which results in a greatly simplified environment (Pimentel 1971). Such monocultures, basically unstable, lack the checks and balances of a natural, diverse ecosystem. Modern agricultural crops, therefore, require constant human care (such as cultivation) and control (with insecticides, rodenticides, herbicides, or all three) if they are to produce as desired.

Replacement of small farms by large farms dependent on mechanization and specialized crop monocultures caused a drastic decline in habitats within and adjacent to croplands. And, because of the decreased crop stability—increased crop vulnerability—resulting from the greatly simplified "agricultural ecosystem," farmers are more and more inclined to view native plants and animals as actual or potential "pests" to their crops. DeLoach (1971,

15

p. 225) summed it up when he defined the goal of intensive agriculture: ". . . is to encourage the growth of a foreign organism, a crop, at a high density and to suppress . . . organisms that might compete with it. . . ."

The erratic economics of agriculture is considered to be the primary impetus behind increasing crop specialization in North America. In addition, governmental influence on modern agriculture that has attempted to maintain low-cost food production has largely made the small, diversified farm uneconomical. Consequently, most have disappeared. In turn, for modern agriculture to survive economically, modifications in farming strategies have been necessary, and drastic changes in land use have resulted.[2]

What are Nature's penalties for ecologically unsound agriculture? One obvious penalty is loss of fertile topsoil. Lowdermilk (1975) wrote, "If the soil is destroyed, then our liberty of choice and action is gone, condemning this and future generations to needless privations and dangers." In 1953 (p. 30), Lowdermilk wrote what has been called the "Eleventh Commandment":

> Thou shalt inherit the Holy Earth as a faithful steward, conserving its resources and productivity from generation to generation. Thou shalt safeguard thy fields from soil erosion, thy living waters from drying up, thy forests from desolation, and protect thy hills from overgrazing by thy herds, that thy descendants may have abundance forever. If any shall fail in this stewardship of the land

---

2. These include:

1. Increased specialization of farms (growing fewer crops in larger fields) that causes amalgamation of small, individual fields.

2. Increased size of individual farms due to large, specialized corporate farms replacing small, diversified family farms.

3. Increased use of modern machinery that is more easily and more economically operated in large fields.

4. Increased clearing of fence rows to gain more land for agriculture (Shrubb 1970, Van Deusen 1978) — 1 mile of fence row may occupy 0.5 acre (Moore et al. 1967).

5. Increased use of large sprinkler irrigation systems that eliminate uncultivated irrigation ditches and their banks.

6. Replacement of uncultivated earthen irrigation ditch banks with concrete.

7. Federal aid to farmers through the Agricultural Stabilization and Conservation Service for various types of land "reclamation."

thy fruitful fields shall become sterile stony ground and wasting gullies, and thy descendants shall decrease and live in poverty or perish from off the face of the earth.

In a very real sense, the dire prediction in Lowdermilk's "Eleventh Commandment" is becoming a reality in many parts of the world, including the United States. As the last few years have shown us, modern agriculture emphasizes high production and high technology, such as expensive applications of fertilizers and toxic pest controls. In addition to continued, extensive soil erosion, such as takes place in the wheat raising country of northeastern Oregon and eastern Washington, the single most widespread source of non-point pollution in our streams, rivers, and groundwater is chemicals from intensive agriculture.

Contamination of our water supply is such a serious problem that the Office of Technology Assessment prepared a 2-volume document on "Protecting the Nation's Groundwater from Contamination" (Maddock et al. 1984). Of the 245 substances known to occur in groundwater, they listed 68 compounds connected with herbicides or pesticides, and the list did not even consider fertilizers, rodenticides, or fungicides used in agriculture.

When a system is so simplified and specialized that it becomes vulnerable to otherwise innocuous native biota, the system's stability has been lost through simplification—a loss of structural diversity and thus interrelated processes that allowed the system to function according to its design. When this happens, we humans try to correct the problem through artificial means, such as chemicals; this rarely works, however, and the chemicals end up contaminating the world's waters and other parts of the ecosystem as well (Myers et al. 1984). Carter and Dale (1974, p. 8) summed it up:

> How did civilized man despoil his favorable environment? He did it mainly by depleting or destroying the natural resources. He cut down or burned most of the usable timber from the forested hillsides and valleys. He overgrazed and denuded the grasslands that fed his livestock. He killed most of the wildlife and much of the fish and other water life. He permitted erosion to rob his farm land of its productive topsoil. He allowed eroded soil to clog the streams and fill his reservoirs, irrigation canals, and harbors with silt. In many cases, he used or wasted most of the easily mined metals or other needed minerals. Then his civilization declined amidst the despoliation of his own creation or he moved to new land.

17

Civilization after civilization has risen on the strength of its natural resources and then fallen as the resources were abused and exhausted. Have we really changed much from this scenario? Are we not still mining our natural resources, such as old-growth forests, wherever they occur—Alaska, Canada, Pacific Northwest, and the tropical rain forests of the world? To mine is defined as: to dig under to gain access or cause the collapse of; to process for obtaining a natural constituent; to seek valuable material. The problem with mining natural resources is that mining, by definition, can only go one way—exploitive extraction without replacement. Mining "renewable" natural resources, by definition, probably makes them "nonrenewable" because mining reinvests none of the natural resource capital into that part of the ecosystem from which it came. I know of no living system that can function indefinitely without a balanced input and output of energy, and mining only takes out. Thus, we are actually mining our own civilization when we undercut the resource base on which it grows.

4. What happens when you simplify a system through "management?" Let's take a look at a forest in the Pacific Northwest. We will begin with an old-growth Douglas fir forest because old-growth is the natural commodity we have been liquidating to "sustain" our yield of woodfiber. An old-growth forest is one successional stage in the continuum of successional stages in a forest cycle; it is, however, the most stable stage—where stability is defined as the ability of a community to withstand catastrophe (Margalef 1969) or to return to its "original" state after severe alteration. Although there have been some attempts to derive an ecological definition of old-growth Douglas fir forests in western Oregon and western Washington (Franklin and Spies 1984; Franklin et al. 1981, 1986), the incalculable diversity of these old forests make a uniform, general description or definition virtually impossible. Inherent in these attempts to define old-growth is the continual recurring discovery that the apparent ecological stability of these old forests in time is related to their diversity.

The attributes of forests are composition, structure, and function. Composition refers to the array of plant and animal species, which includes shifts in abundance as well as presence or absence of species. Structure refers to their arrangement in space and time. Function refers to the ecological processes and the rates at which they occur, such as production of organic matter and cycling of

18

nutrients through the various pathways. Increased or decreased complexity of the pathways that route dead organic material—development or loss of a detrital base for the forest—is one example of a functional change with succession (Franklin et al. 1981, Harris 1984).

Old-growth coniferous forests in the Pacific Northwest developed over long periods essentially free from catastrophic disturbance, such as wildfire. They occupied vast expanses of the presettlement landscape. The elimination of these forests began because they represented both a valuable resource (large volumes of virtually free, high-quality wood) and a hindrance to agricultural development (Franklin et al. 1981). Consequently, their liquidation began early. Today, little old-growth forest exists outside of public lands, and liquidation continues. For example, the first record of logging in what is now the Willamette National Forest occurred in 1875. Ninety percent of the timber cut during the first three decades of this century occurred below 4,000 feet elevation. From 1935 through 1980, the volume cut doubled every 15 years. By the 70's, 65 percent of the timber cut was above 4,000 feet elevation (Harris 1984, Harris et al. 1982).

Old-growth coniferous forests differ significantly from young-growth forests in species composition, structure, and function. Most of the obvious differences can be related to four structural components of the old-growth forest: large live trees, large snags (standing dead trees), large fallen trees on land, and large fallen trees in streams (Franklin et al. 1981). This large, dead woody material is a critical carry-over component from old-growth forests into young-growth forests (Harmon et al. 1986). When snags are removed from short-rotation stands following liquidation of the preceding old-growth, 10 percent of the wildlife species (excluding birds) will be eliminated; 29 percent of the wildlife species will be eliminated when both snags and fallen trees (logs) are removed from intensively "managed" young-growth forests (Harris and Maser 1984). As pieces are continually removed from the forest with the notion of the simplistic uniformity that is termed "intensive timber management," we come closer and closer to the ultimate simplistic view of modern forestry—the plantation or "Christmas tree farm."

What do these four examples have to do with our redesigning Nature's forest? First, in the story of the helicopter, you will remember that the tiny, missing safety wire responsible for the crash was neither obvious nor visible when the aircraft was flying. Where is the safety wire in the forest? The irony is that we won't find it until it is missing and something drastic happens. Second, like the city mayor, we are removing pieces because our prevailing economic models say it's okay even though we have no concept of what the pieces do. Third, we are mining the old-growth forests, and we have exceedingly little understanding of young-growth forests, especially their sustainability over time. We are, however, marching ahead as though we know what we are doing—marching from complex, diverse old-growth forests designed by Nature toward simple, uniform Christmas-tree-like plantations designed by humans. And the reasons we may give for our actions, such as jobs and community stability, do not alter the fact that we may be jeopardizing our forests for lack of data and lack of patience with Nature's design (Myers et al. 1984). Fourth, we think of and "manage" a forest as we do modern agriculture. We simplify (specialize) and intensify with no knowledge of the consequences, straining to have more of everything simultaneously. But at what cost—loss of soil fertility, reliance on chemicals that pollute the land and water, and many acres that may not again grow a forest in the foreseeable future?

As forest management intensifies, it comes closer and closer to merging with intensive agriculture, particularly in three respects: (1) the increasing attempt to purify and specialize the crop tree, (2) the increasing move toward monoculture that decreases forest diversity, and (3) the increasing views of plants and animals that exert any perceived negative impact on crop trees as pests. This view "necessitates" an increasing outlay of capital, time, energy, and materials, such as fertilizers, pesticides, plastic tubing to protect seedlings, etc. Intensified management ensures that many normal biological processes will be viewed as management-created competition that conflicts with product goals and will call for continued artificial simplification of the forest. Already the most ubiquitous and irreversible environmental problem we face is the loss of biological diversity (Nelson 1986; Perry, in press; Perry and Maghembe, in press).

*Nature designed a forest with interrelated processes. We are trying to design a forest based on isolated products.*

We humans focus on products of the forests (woodfiber), not the processes that produce the forest. In this way, we have become the wealthy but foolish man in Buddha's parable:

> Once there was a wealthy but foolish man. When he saw the beautiful three-storied house of another man, he envied it and made up his mind to have one built just like it, thinking he was himself just as wealthy. He called a carpenter and ordered him to build it. The carpenter consented and immediately began to construct the foundation, the first story, the second story, and then the third story. The wealthy man noticed this with irritation and said:—"I don't want a foundation or a first story or a second story; I just want the beautiful third story. Build it quickly."
>
> A foolish man always thinks only of the results, and is impatient without the effort that is necessary to get good results. No good can be attained without proper effort, just as there can be no third story without the foundation and the first and the second stories (Bukkyo Dendo Kyokai 1985, p. 141).

We want the third story (products) without having to deal with the foundation (soil fertility), or the first story (patience with Nature's time table), or the second story (consequences of the cumulative effects we are constantly causing through our improved technology for the harvest and use of woodfiber and our abysmal ignorance about the belowground forest processes).

First, we must understand that every lasting human endeavor, such as sustainable forestry, can only be attained by way of the effort and discipline necessary to get the desired results. Next, we also must understand that Nature has designed everything with an *order* that *must be respected* if we are to succeed in achieving our goals. Again, the Buddha gave us a lesson over 2,000 years ago:

> At one time the tail and the head of a snake quarrelled as to which should be the front. The tail said to the head:—"You are always taking the lead; it is not fair, you ought to let me lead sometimes." The head answered;—"It is the law of our nature that I should be the head; I cannot change places with you."

21

But the quarrel went on and one day the tail fastened itself to a tree and thus prevented the head from proceeding. When the head became tired with the struggle the tail had its own way, with the result that the snake fell into a pit of fire and perished.

In the world of nature there always exists an appropriate order and everything has its own function. If this order is disturbed, the functioning is interrupted and the whole order will go to ruin (Bukkyo Dendo Kyokai 1985, p. 140).

Nature's processes are a product of both structural and functional diversity that operate within Nature's ordered design. We neither see nor trust Nature's order; we only perceive a kaleidoscope of ever-changing relationships that we don't understand because we are focused on the third story—the product—rather than the processes that are critical to maintaining the forest of which the tree is the result. We think we can improve Nature's design so we are redesigning the forest to produce only third stories. Before we begin counting our third stories, however, let us remember that our "improved" design of Nature's forest (for example "genetically engineered super trees") is not even off the drawing board.

> *Nature designed a forest in which all elements are neutral.*
> *We are designing a forest in which we perceive some elements as good, others bad.*

All things in Nature's forest are neutral; Nature assigns no values. Each piece of the forest—be it a bacterium or an 800-year-old Douglas fir—is allowed to carry out its prescribed function, offer its prescribed structure, interact with other components through their prescribed interrelated processes. None is more valuable than the other, each is only different from the other.

When we assign a value to something in the forest, we are beginning to adjust that object in our focus, and as we bring one thing into focus we simultaneously force almost everything else out of focus (Fig. 5). For example, for many years rodents were poisoned in the name of forestry, because we perceived only the "negative" value we "thought we saw"; they ate tree seeds that we wanted to grow. Today we have a different view of forest rodents. Some still eat tree

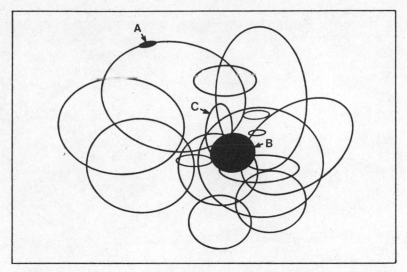

Fig. 5. First we detect something we like in one part of a biological cycle (A) and we assign it a value. Then we isolate it from the rest of the forest and, if possible, learn only those aspects that we want to know (B). When we focus on anything in Nature's forest and assign it a plus or minus (good or bad) value, we develop a myopic view by forcing it into an absolute value (A & B). Our view of its relationships to the interconnected cycles of other things then becomes distorted and out of focus (C).

seeds, but at the same time they disperse viable spores of mycorrhizal fungi, nitrogen-fixing bacteria, and yeast. The following demonstrates the dynamic interactions of the northern flying squirrel in Pacific Northwest coniferous forests as an example of our "new view" for forest rodents.

23

Photo 3. A northern flying squirrel. Flying squirrels cannot fly; they can only glide downward from a higher elevation to a lower elevation. (USDA Forest Service photograph by J.W. Grace.)

## The Squirrel

The northern flying squirrel (Photo 3) is common in conifer and mixed conifer-hardwood forests from the Arctic tree line throughout the northern conifer forests of Alaska and Canada, south through the Cascade Range of Washington and Oregon and the Sierra Nevada almost to Mexico, the Rocky Mountains to Utah, and the Appalachian Mountains to Tennessee (Hall 1981).

The seldom seen, nocturnal flying squirrel is primarily a mycophagist, a fungus eater (Maser et al. 1985a, 1985b; McKeever

1960). In northern Oregon, hypogeous fungi (those fruiting below-ground) and epiphytic lichens (those growing in the tree canopy) are the major foods of the flying squirrel. In northeastern Oregon, for example, hypogeous fungi were the principal food from July to December; from December through June, the lichen *Bryoria fremonti* (Photo 4) was the squirrel's predominant food and also its sole nest material (Maser et al. 1985a). In southwestern Oregon, hypogeous fungi were the major food throughout the year; lichens were not important in the overall diet (Maser et al., 1986).

Photo 4. The lichen *Bryoria fremonti* forms the predominent food of northern flying squirrels from December through June in northeastern Oregon. The squirrels also make their nests of it. (A lichen is a fungus that houses an alga in a mutually beneficial symbiotic relationship; a lichen is thus two plants in one.) (Photograph by author.)

## The Fungus

The term mycorrhiza, literally meaning "fungus-root," denotes the symbiotic relationship between certain fungi and plant roots (Photo 5). Fungi that produce hypogeous sporocarps (belowground fruiting bodies) (Photo 6) are probably all mycorrhizal (Miller 1983; Trappe and Maser 1977). Woody plants in the families Pinaceae (pine, fir, spruce, larch, Douglas fir, hemlock), Fagaceae (oak), and Betulaceae (birch, alder) especially depend on mycorrhiza-forming fungi for nutrient uptake, a phenomenon traceable back some 400 million years to the earliest known fossils of plant rooting structures (Harley and Smith 1983; Marks and Kozlowski 1973; Pirozynski and Malloch 1975).

Photo 5. Mycorrhizae, the symbiotic relationship between certain fungi and plant roots. In this case the fungus forms a mantle, a covering over the roottip. (USDA Forest Service photograph by C.P.P. Reid.)

Mycorrhizal fungi absorb nutrients and water from soil and translocate them to a host plant. In turn, the host provides sugars from its own photosynthesis to the mycorrhizal fungi. Fungal hyphae (the "mold" part of the fungus) extend into the soil (Photo 7) and serve as extensions of the hosts' root systems and are both physiologically and geometrically more effective for nutrient absorption than the roots themselves (Maser et al. 1978a; Trappe 1981; Trappe and Fogel 1977; Trappe and Maser 1977).

Photo 6. The belowground fruiting body (hypogeous sporocarp) of a truffle or false truffle (a fungus). The inner, dark tissue contains the reproductive spores and the light tissue is a tough outer coat. (USDA Forest Service photograph by J.M. Trappe.)

Photo 7. Mold-like threads of fungal tissue, called hyphae, extend from the fungal mantle around the roottip out into the soil where they extract water and nutrients and translocate them into the tree's roots. (Photograph by K. Cromack, Jr.)

## Squirrel-forest Relations

The most obvious squirrel-forest relations are those that occur on the surface of the ground, such as foraging. Even their nesting and reproductive behavior remains relatively obscure because of nocturnal habits. As we probe the secrets of the flying squirrel, however, at least four functionally dynamic, interconnected cycles emerge.

### The fungal connection

The host plant provides simple sugars and other metabolites to

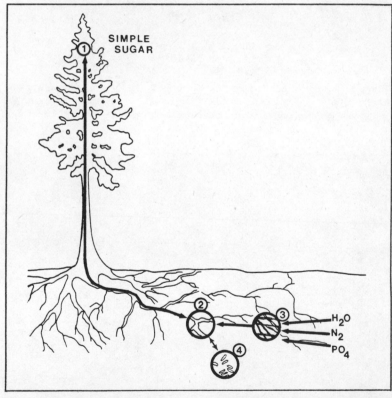

Fig. 6. Nutrient exchange between the tree and mycorrhizal fungus. Tree (1) provides fungus with carbohydrates from photosynthesis. Fungal hyphae extend from the mycorrhizae (2) into the soil (3) acting as an extension of the tree's root system and assisting in uptake of water, nitrogen, and phosphorus. Inside mycorrhizae (2), fungus produces an exudate used as food by bacteria (4) that convert atmospheric nitrogen to a useable form that may move through the fungus into tree roots, trunk, and crown (1).

the chlorophyll-lacking mycorrhizal fungi, which generally are not competent saprophytes (a living plant that derives its nutrients from dead or decaying organic material) (Fig. 6:1). Fungal hyphae penetrate the tiny, nonwoody rootlets of the host plant to form a balanced, harmless mycorrhizal symbiosis with the roots (Fig. 6:2). The fungus absorbs minerals, other nutrients, and water from the soil and translocates them into the host (Fig. 6:3). Further, nitrogen-fixing bacteria (*Azospirillum* spp.) (Photo 8) that occur inside the mycorrhiza (Fig. 6:4) use a fungal "extract" as food and in turn fix atmospheric nitrogen (Li and Castellano 1985). The available nitrogen may be used both by the fungus and the host tree. In effect, mycorrhiza-forming fungi serve as a highly efficient extension of the host root system. Many of the fungi also produce growth regulators that induce production of new root tips and increase their useful lifespan. At the same time, host plants prevent mycorrhizal fungi from damaging the roots. Mycorrhizal colonization enhances resistance to attack by pathogens. Some mycorrhizal fungi produce compounds that prevent pathogens from contacting the root system (Harley and Smith 1983; Marks and Kozlowski 1973; Trappe and Maser 1977).

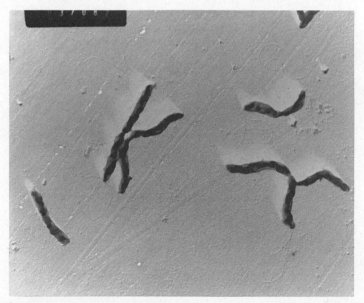

Photo 8. *Azospirillum* spp. is a bacterium that is capable of extracting nitrogen from the air and converting it to a nitrogen compound that plants can use. It is called a nitrogen-fixing bacterium, enlarged 4,700 times. (USDA Forest Service photograph by K. Cromack. Jr.)

Sporocarps (fungus fruiting bodies) are the initial link between hypogeous, mycorrhizal fungi and the flying squirrel. Flying squirrels nest and reproduce in the tree canopy (Fig. 7:1) (Photo 9) and come to the ground at night where they dig and eat hypogeous sporocarps (Fig. 7:2) (Photos 10 and 11). As a sporocarp matures, it produces a strong odor that attracts the foraging squirrel. Evidence

Fig. 7. Northern flying squirrel-forest interaction. The northern flying squirrel nests and reproduces in the canopy (1); it descends at night to the ground to eat hypogeous fungal sporocarps (2).

of a squirrel's foraging remains as shallow pits in the forest soil and occasional partially eaten sporocarps (Photo 12).

Sporocarps of hypogeous fungi contain nutrients necessary for small animals that eat them (Fogel and Trappe 1978; Gronwall and Pehrson 1984; Sanders 1984). In addition to nutritional values, sporocarps also contain water, fungal spores, nitrogen-fixing bacteria, and yeast (Li and Castellano 1985; Maser et al. 1978a, 1985a). As we shall see, they all become important in our forest network.

Photo 9. The northern flying squirrel both nests and reproduces in the tree tops. (USDA Forest Service photograph by J.W. Grace.)

Photo 10. The northern flying squirrel descends at night to the forest floor to hunt for its fungal food. (USDA Forest Service photograph by J.W. Grace.)

Photo 11. A northern flying squirrel digging in the forest floor for its predominent food—the belowground fruiting bodies of fungi. (USDA Forest Service photograph by J.W. Grace.)

Photo 12. A small pit in the forest floor where a squirrel dug out the belowground fruiting body of a fungus and did not eat it. (USDA Forest Service photograph by J.M. Trappe.)

*The squirrel connection*

When flying squirrels eat sporocarps (Photo 13), they consume fungal tissue that contains nutrients, water, viable fungal spores, nitrogen-fixing bacteria, and yeast (Fig. 8:1). Pieces of sporocarp move to the stomach (Fig. 8:2) where fungal tissue is digested, then through the small intestine (Fig. 8:3) where absorption takes place, then to the cecum (Fig. 8:4). The cecum is like an eddy along a swift stream; it concentrates, mixes, and retains fungal spores, nitrogen-fixing bacteria, and yeast (Li et al. 1986, Maser and Maser, unpublished data). Captive deer mice (Photo 14) retained fungal spores in the cecum for more than a month after ingestion (Maser and Maser, unpublished data). Undigested material, including cecal contents, is formed into excretory pellets in the lower colon; these pellets, expelled through the rectum (Fig. 8:5), contain all the viable elements (Li et al. 1986) (Fig. 8:6).

Photo 13. A northern flying squirrel eating a belowground fruiting body of the fungus *Hysterangium* spp. (USDA Forest Service photograph by J.W. Grace.)

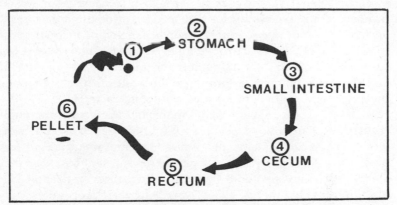

Fig. 8. Passage of sporocarp through the northern flying squirrel: (1) sporocarp is eaten; (2,3) fungal tissue is digested; fungal spores, nitrogen-fixing bacteria, and yeast propagules pass intact; (4) spores, bacteria, and yeast are concentrated and mixed; (5) fecal pellets are formed; and (6) fecal pellets containing viable spores, bacteria, and yeast are passed.

Photo 14. Deer mice are small, nocturnal denizens of the forest. (Photograph by M.L. Johnson.)

*The pellet connection*

A fecal pellet (Photo 15) is more than a package of waste products; it is a "pill of symbiosis" dispensed throughout the forest. Each fecal pellet contains four components of potential importance to the forest: (1) spores of hypogeous mycorrhizal fungi (Photo 16), (2) yeast (Photo 17), (3) nitrogen-fixing bacteria, and (4) like the yolk that feeds the chicken forming in the white of an egg, the complete nutrient component for nitrogen-fixing bacteria.

Each fecal pellet contains viable spores of the mycorrhizal fungi (Kotter and Farentinos 1984; Trappe and Maser 1976), and each fecal pellet also contains the entire nutrient requirement for *Azospirillum* spp. The yeast, as a part of the nutrient base, has the ability to stimulate both growth and nitrogen-fixation in *Azospirillum* spp. (Li et al. 1986). Abundant yeast propagules may also stimulate spore germination because spores of some mycorrhizal-forming fungi are stimulated in germination by extractives from other fungi, such as yeast (Fries 1966; Oort 1974).

Photo 15. Fecal pellets of a northern flying squirrel that act as an ecological pill that helps to inoculate the soil with live fungal spores, nitrogen-fixing bacteria, and yeast. (Photograph by author.)

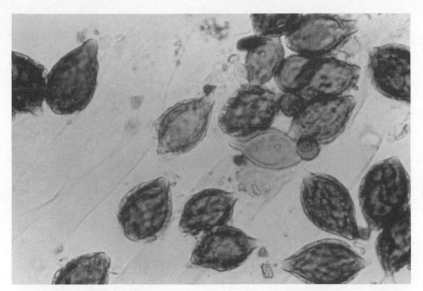

Photo 16. Fungal spores pass unharmed through rodent digestive tracts and germinate. (USDA Forest Service photograph by J.M. Trappe.)

Photo 17. Yeast propagules (white spots) cultured from a fecal pellet of a northern flying squirrel. (USDA Forest Service photograph by C.Y. Li.)

If all this sounds incredibly complicated, that's because it is. And it is only one tiny glimpse of a forest's total complexity. To continue, the fate of fecal pellets varies, depending on where they fall. In the forest canopy, the pellets might remain and disintegrate in the tree tops. Or a pellet could drop to a fallen, rotting tree and inoculate the wood (Maser and Trappe 1984a). On the ground, a squirrel might defecate on a disturbed area of the forest floor where a pellet could land near a conifer feeder rootlet that may become inoculated with the mycorrhizal fungus when spores germinate (Fries 1982). If environmental conditions are suitable and root tips are available for colonization, a new fungal colony may be established. Otherwise, hyphae of germinated spores may fuse with an existing fungal thallus (the non-reproductive part of the fungus) and thereby contribute new genetic material (Trappe and Molina 1986).

Thus we see that the northern flying squirrel exerts a dynamic functionally diverse influence within the forest. The complex of effects ranges through the crown of the tree, down to the soil surface and into the soil mantle where, through mycorrhizal fungi, nutrients are conducted through roots, into the trunk and crown of the tree (Fig. 9), perhaps into the squirrel's own nest tree.

Our world is losing both species and habitats because we are not sensitive to how and why they are functionally interconnected. As emphasized by Rausch (1985), we must understand the organism and habitat in relation to each other if we are to understand the organism, or its function within its habitat. If we do not understand the organism and its function within its habitat, how can we understand the results of unexpected changes in the habitat when the organism is removed?

Dare we assign even a tentative negative value to any organism in a forest if we do not have the slightest idea of its diversity of functions? To assign such a value would be like traveling from New York to Oregon and announcing, "I'm in *the west.*" How far can you travel to the west, before finding yourself in the east, and visa versa? Every perceived value has its precise opposite because one can only be defined in exact relation to the other, and too often as linear thinkers we set out for the west and find ourselves at the opposite end of the compass.

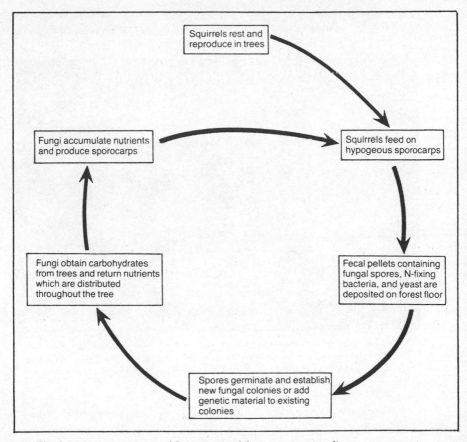

Fig. 9. Major components of flying squirrel-fungus-tree mutualism.

*Nature designed a forest to be a flexible, timeless*
*continuum of species.*
*We are designing a forest to be a rigid,*
*time-constrained monoculture.*

As we have seen, Nature operates in trends—not absolutes. Further, Nature is neutral; She assigns no values, makes no predictions, and cultivates no peptic ulcers over outcomes of constantly changing relationships. In Nature, what is simply is (Photo 18).

Photo 18. A mixed-species stand of trees with western hemlock, western redcedar, and Douglas-fir. We are simplifying the forest to contain almost exclusively one species of tree in any given plantation. (Photograph by L.D. Harris and the author)

We, on the other hand, have defined time and have now become ruled by our construct. Time is defined as: The measured or measurable period during which an action, process, or condition exists or continues; a nonspatial continuum in which events occur in apparently irreversible succession from the past through the present to the future. We have also assigned positive values to items in the forest and view them as desirable products. We must harvest and market a surplus to make a profit. We use time to measure our efficiency in production of salable goods: hence the adage, "time is money."

Under present design strategy, time is a perceived limiting factor on and against which our management decisions are based. The artificial time constraints we place on diverse biological processes in our attempt to create fast, uniform, monocultural crops of trees serves to concentrate and magnify conflicts we perceive in time and space. For example, when we *focus* our attention on a chosen *product*

40

as a measure of the success of our management efforts, we *forget* that a forest encompasses *processes* and has no endpoint. We arbitrarily choose short periods of time as frames of reference within which to manage a normally long-lived forest for selected product(s), and anything diverted to a different endpoint is considered a loss. Such linear thinking ensures conflict and fosters the concept that anything in a forest not used by people is a waste.

The more intense forest management becomes, the less flexible it becomes. The less flexible it becomes, the more stringent time constraints become. The more stringent time constraints become, the more varied, focused, and irreconcilable human conflicts become. This progression of events leads to competition, to human conflict, namely: two or more persons want the same thing (old-growth trees) at the same time on the same acre for different reasons and there are not enough old-growth trees to satisfy both.

The pivotal concept is single-species management under strict time constraints for a particular product that forecloses other amenities that would require a different or greater mix of species and habitats with vastly different time regimes. For example, a mill owner wants to cut a stand of old-growth timber for the potential profit that can be made, and then wants to streamline (redesign) the forest site to continually grow new trees faster so more money can be made. People in a conservation organization want to retain the mixed-species stand of old-growth timber intact through time for a pair of nesting spotted owls (Photo 19). Both parties want the same stand of old-growth trees at the same time on the same acre but for different reasons. The mill owner wants to cut the trees for the profit, and the conservation organization wants them to remain intact and growing to house the spotted owls. Each perceives its purpose to be correct and mutually exclusive.

*Nature designed a forest over a landscape.*
*We are trying to design a forest on each acre.*

Nature designs Her landscapes as ever-changing relationships in time and space. We gaze on them for but an instant; yet past, present, and future are contained in that instant. The intuitive and the rational are brought together, as they were for me seven years ago on Steens Mountain:

41

Photo 19. The spotted owl is closely tied to old-growth forests in the Pacific Northwest. (Oregon Cooperative Wildlife Research Unit photograph by Gary Miller.)

The sky grays, then pales. The last stars twinkle and fade. The east turns pink, then orange, then gold as the sun ascends to the horizon. A light breeze causes aspen leaves to tremble. The world—this high, desert-mountain world—has the crisp, clean, thin odor of autumn.

Cleansed by last night's thunderstorm, the earth accepts the morning sun. Deer feed on mountain sage. A buck, antlers in velvet, lifts his head and looks toward the valley. Sage grouse cluck as they nip flowers. Ground squirrels warm themselves on rocks, and horned larks sit hunched on bare soil as they, too, absorb the warmth.

Nothing do they know of the mighty glaciers that once ruled

Photo 20. A large valley carved out by a glacier during the last ice age. (Photograph by author.)

this high land, that ground the rocks and shaped the valleys (Photo 20), that carved the cirques at each valley's head, and in their passing left hanging meadows and small, clear lakes. They cannot read the fine scratches left by the ancient glaciers' feet on the rounded, polished boulders. They do not know of the glaciers, and they probably do not care. Theirs is the world of today and, perhaps, of tomorrow. And when there is no tomorrow, when their life cycles have been fulfilled, they shall join the glaciers as have the generations before them. Yet each generation and each generation's generation has helped to change the land. In passing, they joined the glaciers, fires, and winds—the artists that sculptured and textured the mountain.

Nature designs her landscapes with single-celled bacteria, mosses, trees, slope, aspect, fire, elevation, glaciers, and volcanos (Photo 21). Her variety and scales are infinite. She covers some of Her landscapes with forests and then uniquely molds each with soils of different parentage, with insects and disease, fire and ice, drought and floods and time.

Nature paints and repaints Her landscapes with all manner of brushes and strokes, from fine and delicate to coarse and bold

43

Photo 21. Nature often designs Her landscapes with volcanos that spread lava over the earth. Note island around which the molten lava flowed. (Photograph by author.)

(Photo 22). We, on the other hand, lack Her imagination, skill, patience, and daring. Our landscapes, conceived in planning rooms, are unimaginative and weak—prone to unravel. The difference? Nature designs over interrelated landscapes; we design a few isolated acres at a time. Nature designs with dynamic processes; we try to design by holding everything constant, including ecological processes.

A few years ago, for example, I was asked to examine black bear damage to trees on the Mt. Hood National Forest. The wildlife biologist said it was severe damage, and indeed it was—the most severe I had ever seen.

We spent most of the day in the field looking at 20- to 30-year-old Douglas fir plantations where black bear had been eating the cambium (inner bark) off the trees. These plantations were on densely forested steep slopes, on gentle slopes, and on flat ground with more widely spaced trees. The bear had climbed the trees on the steep slopes and had eaten the cambium on the open downhill side about two-thirds of the way up the trees. Bear had hooked their claws under the bark of trees on the gentle slope and pulled it off in

Photo 22. Nature designs Her landscapes with all manner of brushes and strokes. Her artistry is ever changing. (Photograph by author.)

great strips (Photo 23). They had then scraped off the cambium with their lower, front teeth (Photo 24)—the type of feeding I am most familiar with (Maser 1967). On flat ground, the bear had had to work hard to get around the low limbs and reach open areas of bark (Photo 25).

Photo 23. Bark stripped off a young Douglas fir by a black bear. The bear hooked the claws of its front foot under the bark and pulled it off. (Photograph by author.)

After four or five hours in the field, the biologist asked, "What can we do?" I answered, "Cut trees differently; that will stop most of the bear damage." "How?" he asked. "Let's go back to the office and I'll show you," I replied. Once in the office, I had him get out all the maps and aerial photographs of the area. Then I showed him that all

Photo 24. Once the outer bark is removed, the bear scrapes the inner bark (cambium) off the stem with upward vertical strokes of its lower incisor teeth. (Photograph by author.)

the clearcuts were within one-quarter mile of one another and were all about the same age. The way the sale units had been laid out had created much open bear habitat within an otherwise dense old-growth forest. The bear population had responded, as would be expected, to the boon of new habitat. As the plantations grew up—all at once—the expanded bear population found itself with a rapidly shrinking food supply, and the bear were forced to supplement their diet with the cambium of plantation trees. The reason I say "forced" is that a bear population also existed outside the plantations, so those bear in the plantations could not move without

Photo 25. A black bear had difficulty maneuvering about the small limbs and an old wound from a bear having injured the tree years earlier to eat the bark. This time the bear could only get at the bark on the scar tissue as it was healing over the old wound. (Photograph by author.)

having to compete with other resident bear. The solution was simple, take the bear's habitat needs and habits into account when planning future timber sales and make appropriate adjustments. We can either create or minimize bear habitat as desired. There is no need to make the same mistake again.

When we are ready, Nature can teach us to be better landscape artists. First, however, we must learn humility, and we have a long, long way to go before our lesson is learned.

*Nature designed Pacific Northwest forests to live*
*500–1200 years.*
*We are designing a forest that may seldom live 100*
*years.*

Although Nature designed forests in the Pacific Northwest to live 1,200 years, and sometimes more (Stoltmann 1987), 400- to 500-year-old forests are more usual. People do not live as long as trees, so it is difficult to conceive the complexity of a tree's life cycle. If a Douglas fir lives 800 years and then takes another 400 years to decompose and recycle into the living forest (Photo 26), one-third of its useful existence is after it dies—as a standing, dead tree (snag) (Photo 27), a fallen tree (Photo 28), or both, which are merely altered states of the live tree.

We could use an 800-year-old Douglas fir to further illustrate the longevity of our forests, but instead we will use only a 500-year-old tree. If a 500-year-old Douglas-fir blows over this year, 1987, and takes 250 years to decompose and recycle into the forest, that represents 10 lifetimes of a 75-year-old person and 25 working careers of

Photo 26. A large, live old-growth Douglas-fir. (USDA Forest Service photograph by J.M. Trappe.)

Photo 27. A large, old-growth snag. (USDA Forest Service photograph by Tom Spies.)

30 years each. Further, that 500-year-old tree would have germinated in 1487, and it would lie on the forest floor decomposing until 2237.

Another way of looking at this is to consider a person who is 50 years old this year, 1987; the person was born in 1937. If we subtract 50 years from 1937, that comes to 1887. If we add 50 years to 1987, that comes to 2037. So, three life times of a 50-year-old person (150 years) spans from 1887 to 2037. Think of our monumental technological advances in that 150 years (3 lifetimes of a 50-year-old person) compared to the little we have learned about the ecological processes that maintain the forests we manipulate! Consider further that if we subtract 150 years from 750 years (the

Photo 28. A large, fallen old-growth Douglas-fir. The man standing next to the fallen tree is about six feet seven inches tall. (Photograph by author.)

length of time it took the tree to complete its cycle), that leaves 600 years unaccounted for . . . 600 years of intense interactions of which we know next to nothing.

Our intent, as we redesign the forest, is to permanently and drastically shorten the life of the trees. In so doing, we are altering the entire dynamics of how the forest functions without the slightest idea, or any data, concerning how such actions will affect the sustainability of the forest (Maser and Trappe 1984b, Maser et al. 1984). To maximize the harvest of woodfiber today, we gamble with the existence of the forests of tomorrow.

> *Nature designed Pacific Northwest forests to be unique in the world—25 species of conifers, 7 major ones, the longest lived and largest of their genera.*
> *We are designing a forest based largely on a single-species' short rotation.*

The following discussion, unless otherwise noted, of Nature's design of Pacific Northwest forests is adapted from Waring and

51

Franklin (1979). Over 40 genera of woody dicotyledons (plants with two seed leaves as opposed to one seed leaf) occurred from Oregon north through Alaska and Siberia to Japan during the early and middle Miocene, 18 to 28 million years ago. A pure coniferous forest, mostly fir, spruce, and hemlock, existed only above 1,625 feet in Japan and above 2,275 feet in Oregon. These forests were therefore widely separated in northwestern North America and northeastern Asia during the early and middle Miocene. They began to occupy large areas by the late Miocene, 12 to 18 million years ago, however, when fir, spruce, and hemlock began to spread through the middle elevations of the western United States, and a continuous coniferous forest extended northward for the first time from Oregon, through British Columbia, into Alaska.

A rich northern forest of spruce, pine, and hemlock—with some larch, fir, beech, oak, and elm—became established in northeastern Siberia during the late Miocene or early Pliocene, 10 to 12 million years ago; a similar trend occurred in Alaska during the same time interval. West of the Cascade Mountains in Oregon, however, an impoverished deciduous hardwood forest of hickory, elm, and sycamore remained during the early Pliocene. As these forests began to shift from deciduous trees to coniferous trees during the late Pliocene, more deciduous trees became extinct than during any period since.

By the early Pleistocene, about 1.5 million years ago, before the major glaciation, the forests of the Pacific Northwest contained the extant species, but it was not until 10,500 years ago that the Douglas fir forests were established much as they are today (Tsukada 1985). The coniferous forests that clothed the landscapes from northern California to the panhandle of Alaska were unrivaled both in size and longevity of individual trees and in the accumulations of living matter (biomass) of individual forest stands. Many of the 25 species of coniferous trees represented the largest and often longest-lived of their genera (Table 1). Extinction of the deciduous hardwood forest of the Pacific Northwest probably was related to climate that favored the conifers. Major components of the original widespread deciduous hardwood forest still persist in Japan, China, Europe, and parts of the eastern United States.

We are redesigning the coniferous forests of the Pacific Northwest based largely on a single-species, short-rotation monoculture that emphasizes the production of woodfiber, not the sustainability of a species-rich forested landscape. Why do we think we can

|  | Typical | | | Maximum | |
|---|---|---|---|---|---|
| Species | (years) | Diameter (inches) | Height (feet) | Age (years) | Diameter (inches) |
| Silver fir | >400 | 36 to 44 | 143 to 179 | 590 | 82 |
| Noble fir | >400 | 40 to 60 | 146 to 228 | >500 | 108 |
| Port-Orford cedar | >500 | 48 to 72 | 195 | — | 144 |
| Alaska-yellow cedar | >1000 | 40 to 60 | 98 to 130 | 3500 | 119 |
| Western larch | >700 | 56 | 163 | 915 | 93 |
| Incense-cedar | >500 | 36 to 48 | 146 | >542 | 147 |
| Engelmann spruce | >400 | >40 | 146 to 163 | >500 | 92 |
| Sitka spruce | >500 | 72 to 92 | 228 to 244 | >750 | 210 |
| Sugar pine | >400 | 40 to 50 | 146 to 179 | — | 122 |
| Western white pine | >400 | 44 | 195 | 615 | 79 |
| Ponderosa pine | >600 | 30 to 50 | 98 to 163 | 726 | 107 |
| Douglas fir | >750 | 60 to 88 | 228 to 260 | 1200 | 174 |
| Coast redwood | >1250 | 60 to 152 | 244 to 325 | 2200 | 200 |
| Western redcedar | >1000 | 60 to 120 | >195 | >1200 | 252 |
| Western hemlock | >400 | 36 to 48 | 163 to 211 | >500 | 104 |
| Mountain hemlock | >400 | 30 to 40 | >114 | >800 | 88 |

Table 1. Typical and maximum ages and diameter at breast height attained by 16 species of coniferous trees on good growing sites in forests of the Pacific Northwest (modified from Waring and Franklin 1979).

"improve" in less than 100 years what it took Nature 28 million years to design and to which we attach so much value?

*Nature designed a forest to be self-sustaining, self-repairing.*
*We are designing a forest to require increasing external subsidies—fertilizers, herbicides, pesticides.*

That Nature designed a forest to be self-sustaining, self-repairing is evident from the exceedingly rich forests we inherited in the Pacific Northwest. It is also evident, that Nature designed a dynamic, timeless forest. Indeed, Nature burned Her forests, ravaged them with insects, froze them with glaciers, and changed them with time, but she always allowed them to heal and to replenish themselves.

We, on the other hand, view forests as a commodity and do not allow them to repair themselves. We seek to exploit, and we thereby miss the lesson Nature tries to teach us:

> "When someone is seeking," said Siddhartha, "it happens quite easily that he only sees the thing that he is seeking; that he is unable to find anything, unable to absorb anything, because he is only thinking of the thing he is seeking, because he has a goal, because he is obsessed with his goal ... ... in striving towards your goal, you do not see many things that are under your nose" (Hesse 1971, p. 140).

And so it is with our management; we see only trees, or big game, or whatever our vested interest is. When we think of Nature's forest as a commodity, we treat it like one (Photo 29). Because we treat it

Photo 29. The way we treat the land is a result of how we think about the land . . . (Photograph by author.)

54

like a commodity, we are trying to redesign it to become one. We take a system designed by Nature to run in 400- to 1,200-year cycles and attempt to replace it with recurring cycles of only the first 80 to 120 years. We do not see the forest. We are so obsessed with our small goals that we neither see nor understand that Nature is warning us about gross simplification by means of outbreaks of the Douglas-fir tussock moth, western spruce budworm, barkbeetles, laminate root rot, blackstain root rot, red ring rot, and other signs. So long as we view the forest as a commodity, we are blind to the gift Nature gave us. And in our blindness, we redesign the forest with an instability that cannot be repaired with fertilizers, herbicides, or pesticides. Our forests can only be healed with humility, love, understanding, and patience.

Part Two

# AS WE THINK, SO WE MANAGE

*All of nature's systems are closed loops, while economic
activities are linear and assume inexhaustible resources
and "sinks" in which to throw away our refuse.*
                                            —Kenneth Boulding

"As we think so we manage" bears the germ of our understanding, of our social consciousness, about Nature. We knew nothing about forestry when North America was settled. Trees were thought of as impediments to agriculture and were removed to expose virgin soil for crops. Our early view of the vast forests was largely negative: they had to be conquered. Then they were viewed as a free, inexhaustible resource (Cox et al. 1985). How do we perceive their value today?

We are still clearing and changing vast areas of the world's forests, but today we do it for a different reason—profit. Forests are no longer cut to be conquered; now they are cut as a commodity to be used or they are considered an "economic waste." The result is the same. Vast areas of the world are being deforested (Dean 1985), and we still argue that we are doing it for the "right" reason. In fact, our argument is the same—*short-term economic expediency*.

Short-term economic expediency, one of humanity's earliest thought and behavior patterns, was seemingly harmless so long as resources were abundant and free for the taking by a relatively small human population. Under such circumstances, the resources that people exploited eventually were restored by Nature. When human use surpassed Nature's yield, the concept of short-term economic expediency became the cause of increasing biological simplification and loss of vigor within the world's ecosystem.

Civilizations have fallen into ruin through the millennia, suffering the consequences of this same decision—to opt for short-term economic expediency. This civilization-killing thought-form stems from two roots: one private, one public. In the first case, a person may own a resource, but does not value it sufficiently to maintain its quality or quantity. In the second case, it is a public resource that no one owns and everyone exploits with the attitude 'If I don't take my share, someone else will." Short-term economic expediency, if it has not been the impetus, is at least a description of the accelerated technological developments in utilization of natural resources.

## Technology, science, and uncertainty

Technology is the application of science, especially to industrial or commercial objectives, the entire body of methods and materials used to achieve such objectives. Broadly, technology is the body of knowledge available to a civilization that is of use in fashioning implements, practicing manual arts and skills, and extracting or collecting materials. As defined, technology is the seed, the germ of human exploitation of the world's resources, including people. Technology has no sensitivity, makes no judgments, has no conscience. It is a human tool and is as constructive or destructive, as conservative or exploitive as its user (Bella et al. 1988a,b).

We did not always know we were ignorant about forestry; too often we still don't. I suspect that, in the beginning, people thought about forestry the way I thought about the beginning of each term in college; I had a perfect, straight-A term—until the first test. Then I had to reconsider. In the beginning of forestry in the Pacific Northwest, people had cross-cut saws, axes, oxen, and horses with which to harvest an apparently unending forest of giant trees. We knew nothing about forests or forestry, so how could we even think about "making mistakes"?

The west was settled, and technological advances in logging equipment and techniques went from flumes, splash dams, and log rafts to log trucks, chainsaws, balloons, and helicopters. Our exploitation of the forests was and is limited only by our technological capabilities; with each advance, therefore, we have the opportunity to expedite harvesting the world's forests. Although on the surface this seems innocuous, even good, we know that each technological advance has one or more hidden trade-offs, such as soil compaction or soil and water pollution, that are not immediately apparent. These hidden trade-offs are really hidden costs in terms of the health and productivity of future forests. We call them cumulative effects.

60

Cumulative effects are not well understood; in fact, most people do not understand the concept. Consider cumulative effects in terms of vintage wine. In my earlier youth, I held the illusion that by keeping careful track of the number of swallows I took of a good wine I would know the limits of sobriety before I crossed the threshold of no return. I could always find the limits of sobriety, but only after I crossed the threshold and knew I had taken one swallow too many. That is a cumulative effect. It is the same in the forest. We only learn about cumulative effects when we see the outcome of our actions—when we have crossed the threshold of no return. The price I paid for crossing the threshold of sobriety was always a horrible hangover that impaired my ability to function until the pollutant was purged and my system was healed. Cumulative effects also impair the forest's ability to function until it is healed.

In an age of rapidly increasing technology, we too often rely on the promise of new techniques to solve problems. We do not question the ecological validity of our profit-oriented goals. To minimize economic trade-offs within an ecological system, we forge ahead in developing new technology, and then we spend inordinate amounts of time and money trying to predict the outcome of trade-offs on our profit margin. At this point we become obsessed with predictability and predictions. Few of us realize how compulsive we are with regard to predictions in our daily lives. We watch or read the weather report even if we don't intend to go out of the house. Many of us let tomorrow's weather prediction decide what kind of day tomorrow will be and how it will make us feel. We face an interesting dilemma in our desire to avoid uncomfortable surprises by predicting the future. In this sense, the only thing we might really predict is our own human behavior. As Sherlock Holmes pointed out to Dr. Watson, "While the individual man is an insolvable puzzle, in the aggregate, he becomes a mathematical certainty." Sherlock goes on to explain that it is impossible to foretell what any individual person will do, but an average number of people are always predictable because, although individuals vary, percentages remain constant (Nierenberg 1981, p. 56). So, while Sherlock Holmes may be correct, that human behavior in some aggregate is a predictable absolute, our problem in trying to predict how the behavior of the forest will influence our profit margins rests not on human behavior but on ever-changing relationships of both living and nonliving components of the forest as part of the ecosystem. Ecological understanding is a non-exact, non-statistical

61

subject. Cumulative effects cannot therefore be rendered statistical, because ecological relationships are far more complex and far less predictable than our statistical models lead us to believe. We cannot foresee the moment when cumulative effects become irreversible.

Our inability to make precise predictions about profit margins and future forestry stems from our growing ignorance (Fig. 10). The

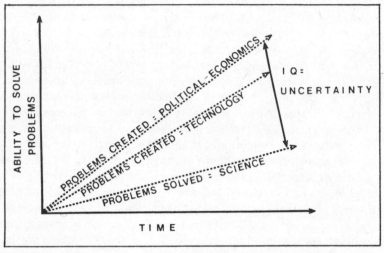

Fig. 10. Technology, driven by short-term political-economics, advances much faster than our scientific knowledge, and the widening gap between the two, our IQ or Ignorance Quotient, causes a great deal of uncertainty in our decisions.

fact that technology for timber harvest and wood utilization, driven by short-term political economics, advances much faster than scientific understanding of how the forest functions is the root of our increasing "Ignorance Quotient" (I.Q.). Add elusive cumulative effects to this equation and our only real "absolute" is a growing uncertainty about the outcome of our decisions. And the more uncertain we are, the more we try to predict and to force results that are within our intellectual comfort zone. None of our efforts, however, can make the forest conform to our simplistic desires for predictable, short-term absolutes, such as sustainable or increasing profit margins, as opposed to Nature's variable-term trends.

## Special cases and common denominators

Sherlock Holmes, in his discussion of the predictability of human behavior, touches the core of special cases and common denominators. He saw each person as a special case and therefore unpredictable, but if we study enough special cases with an eye for their common traits (common denominators), then we can make certain predictions about their behavior. Jung (1958, pp. 16 and 17) put it differently:

> ... Since self-knowledge is a matter of getting to know the individual facts, theories help very little in this respect. For the more a theory lays claim to universal validity, the less capable it is of doing justice to the individual facts. Any theory based on experience is necessarily *statistical;* that is to say, it formulates an ideal average which abolishes all exceptions of either end of the scale and replaces them by an abstract mean. This mean is quite valid, though it need not necessarily occur in reality. Despite this it figures in the theory as an unassailable fundamental fact. The exceptions of either extreme, though equally factual, do not appear in the final result at all, since they cancel each other out. If, for instance, I determine the weight of each stone in a bed of pebbles and get an average weight of 145 grams, this tells me very little about the real nature of the pebbles. Anyone who thought, on the basis of these findings, that he could pick up a pebble of 145 grams at the first try would be in for a serious disappointment. Indeed, it might well happen that however long he searched he would not find a single pebble weighing exactly 145 grams.

We use these same concepts in forestry, but we do not derive as much meaning from them as did Sherlock Holmes and Carl Jung. Take Fig. 11, for example. Each numbered shape above the soil represents an individual stand of trees, a sale unit if you will. Note that each sale unit is a discrete, numbered entity and thus, like an individual human being, is a special case. (Have you ever wanted to be a special case in how other people treated you? Then you know what I mean by special case). Each sale unit (special case) is measured to derive the volume of marketable woodfiber it has produced that we can harvest for a profit. Because we average the volume of each tree, we produce an abstract mean and assign an absolute dollar value to each sale, which is valid precisely once—

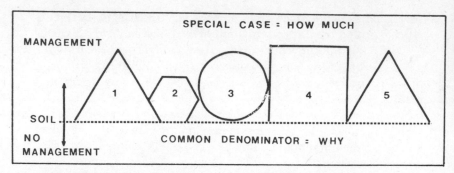

Fig. 11. The individual, numbered shapes above the soil are discrete stands of trees or sale units (special cases). We quantify each to determine how much woodfiber there is and how much it is worth. Note that all of our management is above ground. The soil, one of the common denominators in the forest, tells us why a particular stand of trees grows the way it does. Each stand of trees is only a mirror reflection of the soil's ability to grow it.

now and never again. Once harvested, we expect to plant more trees and derive at least the same volume of woodfiber from those acres (our predictable, artificial, absolute minimum). Whether or not we achieve our goal depends on the "cooperation" of all the variables that constitute the forest.

So long as we think of each stand or sale unit as an isolated special case, we will never understand the forest because a special case is thought to be out of relationship to the whole, which is an aggregate of special cases. We must understand how each delineated stand of trees relates to neighboring stands, to the watershed, and to the landscape before we can begin to understand the forest and make any kind of reasonable predictions about future trends in behavior.

We make two serious, fundamental errors in our view of forestry. First, we fail to realize that all our "management" is what we see above ground (Fig. 11). We do not manage—or even think about or plan for—belowground processes. This brings us to one of the common denominators—the soil (Brown 1981). Each tree, each stand of trees, each forest is only a mirror reflection of the soil's ability to grow that tree, stand, or forest *once*. Second, we assume that the four cornerstones of forestry—the depth and fertility of the *soil* the forest grows on, the quality and quantity of the *water* reaching the forest, the quality of the *air* reaching the forest, and the quality of the *sunlight* reaching the forest—are constants. Because we assume they are constants, they are *omitted* from our economic models and our planning models. Each, however, is a variable of which God gave us only so much working capital. Soil is eroded in two ways, chemically and physically, and we are doing both (Sidle et al. 1985). We pollute our waters and our air with chemicals. Air pollution has a direct effect on the forest and in turn affects the quality and quantity of the sunlight that energizes our forests. *Nothing in Nature is static; She has given us only variables that are constantly changing.*

Now back to the soil for a moment. Freud introduced the notion that our minds contain both conscious and unconscious parts. To me, the soil is our management unconscious, not only because we take it for granted but also because that is where we hide our toxic wastes (Weber and Wiltshire 1985). For example, the melt-down of the nuclear reactor at Chernobyl, in the Soviet Union, early in 1986 was not potentially so dangerous, in my view, as the buried nuclear dump that blew up near Chelyabinsk, in the southern Ural Mountains in the Soviet Union in late 1957 or early 1958. "The land was dead—no villages, no towns, only chimneys of destroyed homes, no cultivated fields or pastures, no herds, no people—nothing. It was like the moon for many hundreds of square kilometers, useless and unproductive for a very long time, many hundreds of years" (Leo Tumerman, quoted in *Corvallis Gazette-Times*, Corvallis, Oregon, 29 April 1986).

We must remember that the soil not only supports all plants growing in it but also supports myriad hidden processes that are necessary for its fertility and for healthy forests. The nuclear accident is only a drastic, faster version of the global soil damage we are accomplishing through the slower, insidious poisons of our management-introduced array of biocides. Ehrlich (1985) wrote, ". . . the ecosystems of this planet generate and preserve our soils. They are not doing such a good job anymore because of the many substitutions human beings have made in ecosystems. ...humanity can perhaps survive the depletion of nonrenewable supplies of fossil fuels, but it certainly cannot survive the current rate of soil depletion." We can only sustain healthy forests by learning about and planning for the special cases (stands of trees) in relation to their common denominators (soil, water, air, sunlight, etc.).

# Short-term economic expediency

Although short-term economic expediency has been a mainstay of human society for millennia, its environmental consequences probably became evident first in the forests of the world. Before we climb back into our time machine to look at some ancient and not so ancient examples of what humanity has done and is doing to the forests of the world, it is important to understand that no human action takes place without first the thought. It is therefore imperative that we understand the thought processes behind our historical journeys, so to keep the text readable and still give you the pertinent flashbacks, I have paraphrased in the text and relegated lengthy quotes to Appendix 2.

## Greece

The effects of deforestation were apparent even in early Greek time. In the time of Homer, for instance, there still were "deep, endless, shadowy" forests, but Greek civilization had already begun to take its toll through woodcutting for shipbuilding, construction of houses and fortifications, and for illumination and heat. The forests were further impacted by livestock grazing, windstorms, and wildfires in the 8th and 7th Centuries B.C. The forests around Athens were finally decimated from years of exploitation for warships, which resulted in severe soil erosion; so the Athenian Empire found the colony of Amphipolis in 436 B.C. But when war erupted between Sparta and Athens, Sparta blocked the timber supply by besieging Amphipolis, which caused the capitulation of Athens in 404. Plato, who lived from 427? to 347 B.C., having survived the war was one of the first to observe, in an altogether brilliant way, the relationships of deforestation, water supply, and soil erosion in the mountainous region of Attica, the hinterland of Athens (Rubner 1985).[3]

---

3. See Appendix 2 for long quote.

We turn next in our recital of ruined lands to Thirgood (1981) and his excellent, fascinating account of "Man and the Mediterranean forest, a history of resource depletion." Although Thirgood discusses the influence of climate in the Mediterranean Basin, Butzer (1961, in Thirgood 1981) concluded that archaeological evidence does not support a hypothesis of climatic deterioration in historical times; rather it indicates the abandonment of wide areas because of economic deterioration, political instability, nomadic incursions, and decline of urban activity. The main agents of deforestation, Thirgood writes, were cultivation, exploitation for timber and fuel (much of it for shipbuilding), industry, wars, population pressures, human-caused fires, and grazing. Thirgood (1981, pp. 46, 47, and 55) concludes:

> Lack of appreciation of the renewable nature of the forest has sometimes led commentators astray. The record clearly shows continuing, and often extensive, exploitation, but it is evident from recurrent reference to the same forested regions that, despite periodic depletion, many of these regions were able to return to productivity. Undoubtedly, rehabilitation was achieved much less by active effort than by general happenstance, but it did occur; it does suggest a low incidence of grazing. As has been shown, there were considerable agricultural clearances and it is probable that timber fellings led to the loss of land to cultivation and grazing, at least for a period, but apart from the early loss of the thin soils of Greece, in most parts of the Roman world an intensive crop husbandry maintained fertility even on cleared slopes, while the remaining forests were able to meet timber requirements. . . .
>
> The overall conclusion is that, despite the considerable inroads, and with the exception of the more arid, thin-soiled conditions, extensive timber forests, though often depleted, still remained at the end of the classical period, and that natural regeneration was able to maintain the forests in being.
>
> During the post-classical period, man continued to collect fuel and use wood for construction. With the revival of civilization and ordered life, requirements increased. Despite the demands of ever-increasing architectural standards, the greatest drain was again shipbuilding. This demand was to continue so long as the world's commerce was carried, and wars were fought, in wooden hulls. The Crusades gave a major impetus to the development of

the shipping of the European Mediterranean states and to the development of their eastern maritime commerce. The great medieval fleets of the Mediterranean powers, the Byzantines, the Turks, the Italian maritime states of Venice, Genoa and other cities, and the pirate flotillas, were launched at the expense of the Mediterranean forest.

The loss, as distinct from depletion, of the Mediterranean forests cannot be ascribed solely to exploitation for timber or, with lesser force, fuel or even to cultivation, for, in the absence of other factors, regeneration and reinvasion might have been expected. Yet it is clear that depletion has been catastrophic. The bare mountains of the readily accessible littoral [ocean shore] are witness that excessive exploitation of the forests initiated the cycle of destruction.

## Middle East

Included in Thirgood's (1981) book is a chapter on "The deforestation of the Levant," the Middle East. He sums up the situation in the opening paragraph (p. 85):

Nowhere more than in the Levant can we find substantial evidence that the deterioration and desiccation of the Mediterranean environment is not the consequence of adverse climatic changes, but of the combination of a vulnerable environment and a long history of man's impact on natural resources; *an impact that has been no less destructive for being gradual and in ignorance of cumulative effects* [emphasis mine]. But also in few other areas has it been as convincingly shown that not only do *we have the ability to destroy our habitat, but also the ability to reclaim, given the will and sociopolitical motivation; and also that hard-won rehabilitation, resulting from many years of dedicated effort, may be set at naught by short-term political disturbance* [emphasis mine].

## Forest Decline

There is now growing evidence of decline in productivity over large areas of intensively managed forests in central Europe (Cramer 1984, Schütt and Cowling 1985), China (Zhang et al. 1980), and North America (Bruck and Roberge 1984, Knight 1987, Sheffield and Cost 1987, Sheffield et al. 1985, Siccama et al. 1982, Zedaker et al. 1987). There is also a sizable body of information from integrative research at the ecosystem level that clearly shows important connections among the wide variety of processes that operate within a forest (Harmon et al. 1986, Maser et al. 1987a, Waring and Schlesinger 1985). Further, there is solid evidence that diversity of plant and animal species (species richness) is a critical factor in maintaining these processes (Franklin et al. 1981, Harris 1984, Li et al. 1986, Maser et al. 1978b, Norse et al. 1986, Trappe and Maser 1977). Where there is a problem there is a cause. The Society of American Foresters (1984) recognized this: "In the face of mounting evidence that forest productivity is declining world-wide, researchers [and managers] know too little about complex ecosystems and the cumulative effect of subtle stresses from atmospheric pollutants." And from the Congress of the United States (1976) came this: ". . . regulations, under the principles of the Multiple-use Sustained Yield Act of 1960 . . . shall include . . . guidelines which . . . provide for diversity of plant and animal communities. . . ." Elsewhere in the act, Congress states, ". . . the Forest Service has both a responsibility and an opportunity to be a leader in assuring that the Nation maintains a natural resource conservation posture that will meet the requirements of our people in perpetuity. . . ."

It is worthy of note that decades of scientific research have concentrated on every possible cause of forest decline *except* that it might be the direct result of intensive plantation management based on ignorance of forest processes. The forests of central Europe are now dying; in fact, West Germany recently (1986) issued a postage stamp "save our forests in the eleventh hour." *And yet the effects of a century or more of intensive management based on short-term economic expediency are seldom discussed* (Zengerle and Allan 1987). Schütt and Cowling (1985), for example, list a variety of reasons for *Waldsterben* (the dying forest); not one of them is directly connected to intensive management. They state that, "The stress factors inducing the *Waldsterben* syndrome are not known, but it is widely assumed (and we believe correctly so) that atmospheric deposition of toxic, nutrient, acidifying, and/or growth-altering substances is involved." And I agree; however, the six general hypotheses put forth to explain one portion of the syndrome or another do not consider the cumulative effects of intensive management. The six hypotheses are listed as: acidification/aluminum toxicity, effects of ozone, deficiency of magnesium, general disturbance of physiological function, excess atmospheric deposi-

69

tion of nutrients (especially nitrogen), and air transport of growth-altering organic substances.

In fact, the cause or cause(s) of *Waldsterben* in central Europe are generally seen as occurring from outside the forest, and we hear much about acid rain (Butzke 1984). "One German scientist even believes a 'mysterious virus imported from Czechoslovakia' triggered *Waldsterben* (Forrester 1986). Deumling (1986), who is responsible for environmental affairs of a timber company based in Wissen, West Germany, wrote:

> We in West Germany have more evidence and certainly more severe forest damages and therefore feel that it is only prudent to advocate a reduction of the air pollution load we receive even though all the facts are not in and probably never will be. The forest is too complicated an ecosystem to ever be fully explained in all its components.
>
> I do have to wonder how somebody who is responsible for "maintaining healthy forests" for his company [in the United States] can, with admittedly insufficient evidence, exclude the possibility that air pollutants—among them sulfur dioxide—are harming his forests, while his colleagues across the Atlantic [in West Germany] have wholeheartedly endorsed such an effort [to reduce sulfur dioxide and nitrogen oxide].

Schütt and Cowling (1985) concluded their article by stating that there is much concern amongst scientists and the public at large that the forests of central Europe "may not be sustainable." They reiterate that atmospheric deposition of chemicals may be involved and ask for help in understanding ". . . one of the most remarkable forest disease problems of this century." Again, I agree that atmospheric pollutants may well be playing a role in *Waldsterben*. Yet I cannot help but wonder how the cumulative effects of a century or more of intensive plantation management and use may have strained the forests of Central Europe, and thus predisposed them to the *"Waldsterben* syndrome" we see today.

Only a few papers have examined other aspects of central European forests. Cramer and Cramer-Middendorf (1984) examined the correlation of climatic factors and damage to central European forests since 1851. Plochmann (1968) pointed out some cumulative effects of intensive management, and Hill et al. (1975) summarized some cumulative effects of silvicultural practices on soil invertebrates in both central European and North American forests. There are numerous groups of soil animals that, together, may have a greater number than aboveground animals (Hill et al. 1975), and they may be disproportionately important with respect to cycling and release of plant nutrients (Macfadyen 1961).

In the past, lime has been applied to the forest soils in Germany in an attempt to reduce their acidity. Franz and Loub (1959) found that they could still detect the changes in population structure between tiny soil plants and small soil animals 50 years after an application of lime. The small soil animals, such as mites, are dependent on the tiny soil plants, such as bacteria and algae, for energy and these tiny soil plants are in turn affected by the numbers of small soil animals that eat them; so a change in one effects a change in the other. Franz and Loub also found that the population density of mites was half the population in control plots 26 years after application of a mixture of fertilizer and lime. That fertilizers usually increase the numbers of small soil animals is often interpreted as beneficial, but we are only now learning that the optimum is invariably below the maximum, so more is not necessarily better (Hill et al. 1975).

One aspect of intensive forestry in central Europe that is seldom discussed is simplification. Figure 12 (A) represents an unmanaged, mixed deciduous-conifer European forest; note the mix of structural shapes of the trees (that would include different species and ages) and the "woody material" on and in the soil. The belowground processes are fully functional in the unmanaged forest compared to the grossly simplified, intensively managed stand with only one even-aged species of tree and no woody debris left in the system. Such simplification is a product of ". . . hundreds of years [in which] all timberland has been cut, grazed, and raked for litter" (Plochmann 1968). He later stated that the forests have been "overcut, overgrazed, overraked. . . ." (Photos 30 and 31) What it took Europeans centuries to do to their forests, it is taking us less than 200 years to accomplish—one-third the life of a 600-year-old Douglas fir. The only difference in the speed of modern deforestation that I can see is that we have technology that was unavailable 100 years ago. I say deforestation because, as Plochmann (1968, pp. 24 and 25) said of the German forests (our model), "It took about one century for them [negative biological consequences of intensive forestry] to show up." He further stated that, "Many of the pure stands [of spruce] grew excellently in the first generation but already showed an amazing retrogression in the second generation."

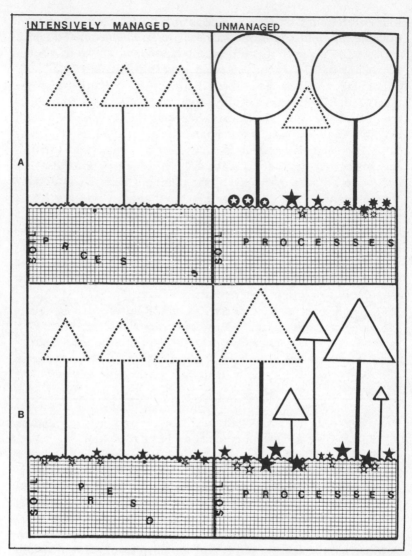

Fig. 12. A of this schematic represents the forests of southern Germany. The intensively managed Norway spruce forest exists today, as opposed to the original mixed conifer-hardwood or deciduous hardwood forests of European beech, oak, hornbeam, linden, and other species (Cramer 1984). The symbols on and in the soil of the unmanaged forest represent woody debris, from large fallen trees to branches one inch or greater in diameter. These are missing from the soil of intensively managed stands. B of this schematic represents the forests of the Pacific Northwest. The intensively managed forest of 70- to 80-year-old Douglas-fir depicts the future in which there will be little woody debris on or in the soil, unless it is left on purpose. The original old-growth forests often consisted of mixed-species stands and much woody debris, ranging from large, fallen trees to small branches.

Photo 30. The German people keep the floor of their plantations clean of woody material. (Photograph by author.)

Photo 31. Woody material and even twigs, gleaned from the forest floor in Bavaria, West Germany, end up in the fire place. (Photograph by author.)

Although the cause or causes for the decline in forest productivity may not be readily apparent, some possibilities come to mind. I do not usually care for acronyms, but the one for "short-term economic expediency" (SEE) has more than the usual aptness. Short-term economic expediency is the common denominator behind intensive, exploitive use of the world's resources, and the acronym *SEE* reminds me that in renewable resources we *manage* only what we *see,* and what we see is only what occurs *above* ground. Worster (1979, p. 6) has defined the capitalist approach to the land in jarringly stark terms, inviting us to look beyond the forest into our cultural ethic for the roots of the growing ecological dilemma:

> The land in this culture, as in any other, is perceived and used in certain, approved ways; there are, in other words, ecological values taught by the capitalist ethos. We may sum them up in three maxims.
>
> 1. *Nature must be seen as capital.* It is a set of economic assets that can become a source of profit or advantage, a means to make more wealth. Trees, wildlife, minerals, water, and the soil are all commodities that can either be developed or carried as they are to the marketplace. A business culture attaches no other values to nature than this; the nonhuman world is desanctified and demystified as a consequence. Its functional interdependencies are also discounted in the economic calculus.
>
> 2. *Man has a right, even an obligation, to use this capital for constant self-advancement.* Capitalism is an intensely maximizing culture, always seeking to get more out of the natural resources of the world than it did yesterday. The highest economic rewards go to those who have done the most to extract from nature all it can yield. Private acquisitiveness and accumulation are unlimited ideals, impossible to satisfy once and for all.
>
> 3. *The social order should permit and encourage this continual increase of personal wealth.* It should free individuals (and corporations as collective individuals) from encumbrances on their aggressive use of nature, teach young people the proper behavior, and protect the successful from losing what they have gained. In pure capitalism, the self as an economic being is not only all-important, but autonomous and irresponsible. The community exists to help individuals get ahead and to absorb the environmental costs.

Although one may not wish to characterize all of capitalism in just this way, it is certainly possible to define much of the current environmental degradation as stemming from the misapplication of the spirit of capitalism. The environmental costs of the purely self-indulgent elements of the capitalistic system outlined by Worster is rapidly destroying the world's natural resources. I will illustrate this point primarily with two examples: intensively managed forests in southern Europe and intensively managed forests in the Pacific Northwest.

Viewing world forests from a position of short-term economic expedience dictates a narrow perspective, a view that includes the notion that soil fertility, quality and quantity of water, quality of air, and quality of sunlight—all of which continuously interact with the forest—are constant. In addition, this view demands gross simplification of the forest for maximum, immediate profit and leaves the future of the forest to the future because any commodity that is not used for today's profit is seen as an economic loss. No provision is made to reinvest any capital in the maintenance of a healthy forest to safeguard the option for the future.

## Europe

First we will examine a generalized view of central European forests. Mid- and low-elevation forests in central Europe historically were either deciduous hardwoods (Photo 32) or mixed deciduous hardwoods and coniferous softwoods (Fig. 12) (Photo 33). As quoted in Cramer (1984, p. 99):

> In the natural forest society where Man had not yet intervened, deciduous trees occupied about ¾ of the forested area; European beech and oak, often together with common hornbeam and linden constituted the main tree species. In the North, the birch was also found in many areas. The oak grew especially well on the more nutrient-rich soils, establishing excellent stands of trees where climatic conditions were more favourable. The beech, with its more modest requirements of site and climate, covered large areas, and also populated the growth zones above the natural oak line. Many different and vigorous tree species growing on meadows constituted the vegetation cover along the river valleys. . . .
> . . . there was a decline in the incidence of pure stands of deciduous trees. Under more favourable conditions of climate and site, vigorous mixed stands appeared there on great areas of the medium slopes, in which Norway spruce, silver fir, beech and, in part, also Scotch pine—in various percentages—were incor-

Photo 32. Deciduous hardwood (European beech) forest in Bavaria, West Germany. (Photograph by author.)

porated. In addition, Scotch pine and oak together formed a mixed type of stand characteristic of the South German landscape. At the higher altitudes—just as in the Highlands of the Harz Mountains—stands of pure Norway spruce were already appearing. Moreover, in the mixed forest of the mountains, the spruce was predominant and, chiefly in the Alps, formed pure stands at something more that 1,300 m [4,225 ft] altitude, which then extended over into the mountain pine regions (BML 1976).

The following brief history of European forests is from Cramer (1984).

When humans arrived in central Europe, changes in the forests were at first quantitative (cutting wood and clearing land for agri-

Photo 33. Mixed deciduous hardwood and coniferous softwood forest in Switzerland. (Photograph by author.)

culture) and then qualitative (changing species composition and converting sites from hardwoods to softwoods). This scenario resulted in the better soils being put to agricultural uses and the poorer soil left in forests. By the end of the Roman era, for example, about a quarter of the land in West Germany had been cleared for agriculture and attendant communities.

Clearing of land in connection with urban and monastic settlement policies began in the early Medieval Period and was considerably intensified during the 11th and 12th centuries, which resulted in the present partitioning into fields and forests. The forests that had served as the most important source of energy and raw materials for a growing and increasingly efficient work-specialized society were reduced to approximately one-third their original extent during this time. Specialized uses of trees began increasingly to change the species composition of the forest. The natural resources of the forests had been exploited to the edge of economic collapse by the end of the 15th century, and the iron producers of the 16th century could not maintain production because they could not get wood. The "great wood crisis" became the limiting economic factor with the rise of manufacturing in the 18th century.

The critical shortage of wood by the end of the 18th century finally forced the change to a planned forest economy. Deciduous hardwoods were replaced with conifers, mainly Norway spruce and Scotch pine, in an effort to stock devastated areas with productive stands as quickly as possible and without incurring financial

Photo 34. Pure conifer plantation (Norway spruce) in Bavaria, West Germany. (Photograph by author.)

risks (Fig. 12) (Photo 34). The criteria for this decision were: (1) easy establishment of a stand, (2) shorter rotations, (3) more rapid growth, especially of Norway spruce, (4) better uniformity of the stands, (5) greater percentage of usable woodfiber, (6) better technology for utilization of woodfiber. The possibilities for exploitation and maintenance of the forests caused a virtual reversal of the original proportions of approximately 75 percent deciduous trees and 25 percent conifers. The forests of the German Federal Republic today are about 70 percent conifers and 30 percent deciduous trees. Of all species of trees, Norway spruce covers 40 percent of the area and Scotch pine covers 26 percent.

The short-term economic success of this forest conversion was and is extraordinary. From 1860 to the present, there has been a clear improvement in supplying the domestic market with wood, and there has been a general stabilization in the wood-related economic situation. These circumstances, for the first time, caused financial criteria to be applied to forestry in striving for a "modest" interest on land capital. *"From this effort, during the 19th century, the theory of financial rotation [rotation age] developed, in which the economic aspect of forestry was given a clear priority"* [Emphasis mine] (Cramer 1984, p. 102). Despite the enormous economic success, grave reservations about the vast monocultures of Norway spruce were expressed early and have never been completely silenced. The arguments, in the final analysis, "are . . . focused on whether the strong preference for Norway spruce, which constitutes the financial backbone of forestry ('bread and butter tree'), is consistent with the requirements of site suitability and stability" (p. 102). In this connection, Cramer (pp. 102–103) states:

> In the utilization of the soil, in many cases, an improved yield is paid for with an increase in production risks. It is . . . the responsibility of management to weigh risks reasonably against utilization or to meet the risks on the same level of scientific knowledge that the rise in yield has made possible. In the event of the intensification- and, in part, rationalization of forestry, a series of special features emerges:
>
> The unusually long productive times grant a clear priority to the aspect of production stability since a single incidence of damage in the course of 80-, 120- or 160-years can endanger the success of the entire operation;
>
> During these productive times, an extension of scientific knowledge is to be expected. The application of improved knowledge to production processes, such as managing of already established forest stands according to stipulated goals, is often difficult. In most cases, up to the time of maturity, intervention can be employed only to modify a program but not to make fundamental changes;
>
> The conditions of production can be basically altered within one forest generation. That has made itself decisively felt, especially in the sector of labour and, thereby, in the expenditures for tending operations;
>
> The demands placed on the forest can change considerably within one productive period. This is valid not only with reference to the lumber market and its demand for specific assortments, but also with a view to the changing interpretations of the forest function, for example, the question of whether maximum

forest production is required or whether the so-called indirect forest functions are to be favoured, i.e., recreation function; ecological functions;

The principle of sustained yield, which postulates the idea of a forest continuing to produce perpetually, requires not only an accommodation of cutting to forest growth, but also the maintenance of the yield capacity of the site. The knowledge that every form of production from the biomass has a considerable influence on the soil dynamics raises the question of whether this tending of the site can be regulated through the planted stand alone.

Generally speaking, intensive management of conifers, especially Norway spruce and Scotch pine, presents many more problems than does any species of deciduous tree. Conifers, for example, are practically the only trees in central Europe to be seriously threatened by forest "pests," such as the pine looper moth, pine beauty, pine moth, Nun moth, saw flies, bark beetles, pine needle cast fungus, pine blister rust, honey fungus, red rot, and a complex of other species of fungi in Norway spruce (Cramer 1984). In fact, Germany's forests are so strained that conifers must have their bark peeled off when cut to avoid outbreaks of bark beetles (Photos 35 and 36).

Photo 35. Logs from coniferous trees are peeled on site to avoid attracting bark beetles that attack stressed trees. (Photograph by author.)

Photo 36. Because most of the intensively managed European conifer plantations are so strained ecologically, logs left in the plantations must have their bark removed to avoid outbreaks of bark beetles that would kill live trees. (Photograph by author.)

Richard Plochmann (1968), a professor at the University of Munich and District Chief of the Bavarian Forest Service at the time he wrote "Forestry in the Federal Republic of Germany," gave a similar, although less exhaustive, picture to that provided by Cramer (1984). Plochmann (1968, pp. 24 and 25) wrote about intensive forestry:

> . . . The calculations made 150 years ago without our modern knowledge and the help of yield tables, site maps, and so on proved to be exact in one regard. . . . The economic superiority of the softwoods over the hardwoods is an indisputable fact.
>
> The biological consequences are less pleasant. *It took about one century for them to show up clearly. . . . Anyway, the drop of one or even two or more site classes during two or three generations of pure spruce is a well-known and frequently observed fact. This represents a production loss of 20 to 30 percent* [emphasis mine][4].

Plochmann (1968, p. 45) concluded his discussion of "The Economic Situation of German Forestry" as follows:

---

4. See Appendix 2 for long quote.

Our forestry will be carried on even under bad economic situations. *We could better the return if we would be willing to give up the high intensity now maintained or if we gave up the principle of sustained yield. We cannot do both and do not want to do either* [emphasis mine]. The first seems imperative for the multiple uses of our forest and the second for the benefit of following generations. . . .

## Asia

Europe is not alone in its forestry problems. In China, a plantation of pure Chinese fir cannot be initiated more than two or three times on the same site; after two or three 20- to 30-year rotations, the soil is no longer able to support the normal growth of Chinese fir (Zhang et al. 1980).

*The Oregonian,* Portland, OR (16 February 1986) carried a story by Kunda Dixit about forestry in Nepal. Dixit wrote:

> Thousands from around the world flock to Nepal each year to witness its spectacular mountain scenery. But when they lower their gaze, the glory fades and yields to a darker sight. Nepal is destroying itself.
>
> Runaway deforestation threatens to transform the Himalayan foothills, ecologists warn, and turn the green landscape of Nepal into a desert. Once isolated and now open to the world, Nepal is falling victim to a world disease: Environmental self-destruction. . . .
>
> Once the trees go, nothing holds the topsoil on the steep hillsides. Every year the rains wash some 3 billion cubic feet of Nepal down to the Bay of Bengal. Soil has become the kingdom's No. 1 "export." . . .
>
> In centuries past, life was better. Nepali villages used to manage their communal woods themselves, and local leaders enforced rotational grazing to prevent the stripping of pastures. But with the nationalization of forests in 1957, and rising population pressures, the balance between man and nature went away.

A point of interest here is that, while working in Nepal in 1966–1967, I visited both the logging camps and the sawmill (located in Trisuli), and I found that the United States AID mission was responsible for Nepalese logging practices and philosophy. We taught them how to log and mill their forests based on short-term economic expediency, but we did not teach the Nepalese about soil conservation or reforestation.

What brand of nationalistic arrogance makes us think we are a special case, that we can ignore the warnings Nature is giving us? Our forestry is patterned after German forestry; our philosophy and practices are also based on and driven by short-term economic expediency. And already in this comparatively youthful country we may be starting to reap some of the same consequences as those sickening the forests of central Europe and China. "The growth of Southeastern pine forests—one of the nation's largest sources of wood—is declining mysteriously after decades of increase. . . ." (Goeller 1986). Shigo (1985, p. 668) in an article on "Wounded forests, starving trees" stated that "Dying forests are nothing new, especially in the northeastern United States." He goes on to say:

> Acid rain, insects, and fungi, are real problems that can kill trees. Wounded forests and starving trees are also realities and part of the total picture. Forest decline is a many-sided problem, yet recent attention has focused on only a few factors. The blame for diebacks and declines cannot be placed on well-publicized short-term agents. Knowing how a tree or forest dies is as important as knowing the causal agent . . .
>
> Trees suffer more than mechanical wounds to trunks and roots. Injuries can also be caused by soil compaction, alteration of drainage patterns, disruption of niches for soil microorganisms, disruption of nonwoody and woody plant species composition. The list goes on.
>
> Starving trees face limitations other than water, oxygen and other chemical elements, and energy. Trees may also starve because of space reduction. As storage space for energy reserves in the tree decreases, so do reserves. Trees can starve in the midst of plenty if storage space is reduced sufficiently.

Now let's take a look at what we are doing to forests in the Pacific Northwest (Fig. 12-B). Note the mixed stand of conifers in the unmanaged forest and remember that Nature designed Pacific Northwest forests to be unique in the world—25 species of conifers, 7 major ones, the longest lived and largest of their genera (Waring and Franklin 1979). These systems also have much woody debris (Franklin et al. 1981, Harmon et al. 1986, Maser et al. 1987a). Upon this richly diverse page of Nature, with all its footnotes and fine print, we are designing a forest based largely on a single-species short rotation (Fig. 12-B, intensively managed). In so doing we are grossly simplifying forest systems. We are speeding up early successional stages as much as possible and liquidating mature and old-growth stages. We are eliminating snags and down woody material over time as we emphasize short-term economic expediency instead of sustainable forest diversity and stability (Harris 1984, Harris and Maser 1984, Harris et al. 1982, Spies and Cline 1987). Intensively managed stands (Fig. 12-B) have little or no wood in the system.

Although our forests may never look as "neatly groomed" as European forests because of our diverse, rugged topography, our economic philosophy is essentially the same. After all, Gifford Pinchot, our first U.S. Chief forester, was trained in Germany. This philosophy of short-term economic expediency is epitomized by John B. Crowell, Jr.—past assistant U.S. Secretary of Agriculture for Natural Resources and Environment— (1986) who stated:

> . . . I do not comprehend how forest plans can propose reductions in harvest levels if the economic analysis required by the National Forest Management Act has been appropriately carried out and given full consideration in arriving at preferred alternatives.
>
> I am, quite frankly, shocked that the Forest Service, which represents itself as being a professional land-managing agency, can possibly even be considering plans so shirking of both good fiscal management and good forest management.
>
> The forest plans must provide for adequate levels of timber harvest if the national interest in having plentiful supplies of wood products at reasonable prices is to be realized and if wood manufacturing mills here in the Pacific Northwest are to be kept operating.
>
> If the plans that are ultimately adopted by the Forest Service provide only for decreased levels of harvest, any attempt by Congress subsequently to fund annual timber-sale programs at harvest rates greater than the plans allow can be frustrated by environmentalist-initiated court actions.
>
> Congress, of course, could overrule the entire planning process. But the political possibilities of achieving such a correction to a planning process gone haywire obviously would be very difficult.

J. Laurence Kulp, Vice President of Technology Strategy for Weyerhaeuser Co., was reported in the *Corvallis Gazette-Times,* Corvallis, OR (19 June 1985) as saying: ". . . new management practices between now and then [the year 2020] will double the amount of wood harvested per acre. . . . Tissue-culture technology and genetic improvements will produce faster-growing, hardier trees that are resistant to insects and disease," he said. ". . . To keep costs down," he added, "it will be important to utilize 'all above-ground biomass,' such as tree stumps, for energy or new products." And studies are still funded like that of Cain and Yaussy (1984, p.12) that conclude: "On a commercial basis it would be hard to justify the intensive hardwood control treatments applied in this study. However, the variety of treatments suggests the degree of disturbance that can be used in uneven-aged stands for controlling hardwoods while, at the same time, favoring pine management. . . . But, short of soil sterilization, complete eradication of hardwoods is unachievable."

Finally, Lovell (1986) wrote an article in *Tomorrow's Forest* about Con Schallu, a research economist with the USDA Forest Service in Oregon, and I quote:

> What does Schallu see as a "best case" scenario for the future? "First of all, the land base dedicated to timber production would stabilize. . . . Furthermore, all forest landowners would accelerate intensive forestry. That means, for example, more use of genetically superior planting stock, pre-commercial thinning, and fertilization. Such a scenario would help encourage the industry to continue to invest in new logging and processing techniques that would result in lower prices for their products."
>
> And what about the "worst case" scenario? "A continual reduction in the land base and a hesitation on the part of the forest industry to commit necessary funds to improve technology. . . . In the worst case, costs would increase and the forest products industry would find it increasingly difficult to compete with substitute building materials: brick, stone, steel, and plastics. Since the production and use of wood products is less energy demanding than its substitutes, the worst case scenario could put a damper on the nation's effort to become energy independent."

Again, the point to keep in mind is that those who say we can intensify plantation management and woodfiber utilization and thereby have more woodfiber are *assuming* that reproduction and growth of trees is the primary or only variable and that *the four cornerstones of forestry—soil, water, air, and sunlight—are constants*. As our forests are simplified aboveground in an attempt to maximize profits through short-term economics, they are simultaneously simplified belowground through alteration of the soil, root, nutrient cycling, and nutrient uptake processes (Blaschke and Bäumler 1986, Brauns 1955, Maser et al. 1987b, Phillips and Van Lear 1984) (Fig. 12). Thus, Nature "balances the books" to the eventual impoverishment of both the forest and the profit margins. Shigo (1985) summed it up:

> Predisposition results from stress—a reversible condition—which means that energy reserves are lowered, and the stage is set for 'strain'—an irreversible condition [such as may now exist in the forests of central Europe]. Energy is required to fuel biological machinery of the tree: to build cells, maintain living functions, reproduce, and defend the tree after injury and infection.
>
> Survival of all living things depends on energy, space to grow, concentrations of water and chemical element, temperature, time, and genetic capacity to resist stress and strain. Because trees cannot move, all these survival factors are linked. Trees either grow on suitable sites, adapt to unsuitable sites, or die. Because survival factors are linked, any disruption in one affects the others.

## Of automobiles and forests

Everything that runs, runs on energy—from automobiles to forests. If a car or a forest is otherwise in satisfactory working order, then it will be "good to the last drop" of energy. If you remember that old Maxwell House coffee slogan, you probably also recall the early models of the Volkswagen bugs, and you will remember that they lacked a fuel gauge so you carried a wooden stick to poke into the gas tank to measure the amount of fuel. This was often a critical exercise because the small "reserve" that you switched to when the automobile seemed to be out of gas might not get you to the next gas station. Today's VW bugs, with their automatic fuel gauges, have taken much of the adventure out of travel into places of unknown gas stations.

Now consider yourself. Have you ever run out of "gas," been hungry and exhausted? When did you notice that you were getting low on energy? You know you are getting low on energy when hunger or fatigue, your fuel gauge, warns you that you have crossed an invisible threshold and need to refuel.

Now consider a forest. It, like you, has an invisible threshold of energy, but unlike yours, you cannot feel the forest's threshold because it is outside of you. And, unlike an old VW bug, there is no place to put a stick to gauge the amount of available fuel.

If you think about it, we spend much or most of our lives gauging things; we call it measurement. We gauge our finances, the gas in our automobile, how far we want to walk, how long to watch TV, how much to eat and drink, when to go to bed, when to get up, and on and on. We must have learned something of value from all of this gauging. We can ask, for example, what are some of the differences between an automobile, a human body, and a forest? What are some of the similarities?

1. An automobile has no living parts; a human body and a forest do. It takes a certain amount of the available energy to keep the living parts in working order; this means that something less than 100 percent of the energy is actually available to move the body or forest forward. Put another way, a living organism (a human body or a forest) has three options: a surplus energy budget that allows growth and forward motion, a maintenance budget that simply keeps it alive and functioning, or a deficit budget with which it cannot maintain itself and begins to decline. (The excellent discussion of energy budgets in deer by Leckenby et al. [1982] is an example of how this dynamic can work) (Fig. 13).

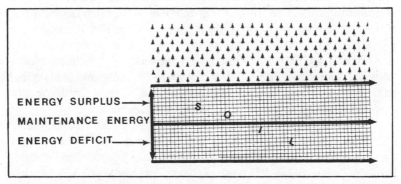

ENERGY SURPLUS——>

MAINTENANCE ENERGY

ENERGY DEFICIT——>

Fig. 13. Where is the magic management line in the forest called the maintenance energy threshold where inputs and outputs of energy—with intact functional processes—must balance for survival of the forest?

2. An automobile can run out of gas without dying. It has no threshold of life or death, but human bodies and forests do. We

87

know where that threshold is for a human body, but we do not know where the threshold is for a forest.

3. When an automobile runs low on fuel, a gauge warns us. We, and others, know something is amiss when we get hungry, tired, or cranky. More important, it takes only a few minutes, hours at most, for the symptoms to manifest themselves, and when they do, we know how to fix them. With a forest, however, it's a different story; it often takes decades, even a century or more, for the "cranky" symptoms to show up, and when they do we don't know what they mean or what caused them.

4. An automobile has many gauges that appear to measure the function of discrete parts of the engine, such as an oil pressure gauge, gas gauge, temperature gauge, battery gauge, etc. Our body, however, has only one gauge to measure everything. It's called "how we feel," and we must learn to interpret that. We don't always succeed. The forest, like the human body, also appears to have one gauge to which all others are joined—its energy-process maintenance threshold. This is the critical balance between the inputs and outputs of energy that keep the vital processes healthy and functioning. We can neither see nor feel this threshold (Fig. 13).

5. How we use an automobile, our body, or the forest determines how fast the fuel is used up and how soon the processes are worn out. The more "conserving" we are, the longer each lasts; the more we abuse them the faster they wear out. An automobile can be rebuilt indefinitely so long as a single original part remains functional; of course, it will not be the same automobile. We can have parts of our body replaced also, but our bodies cannot be totally rebuilt and so may be increasingly limited in function, a non sequitur in this instance. A forest cannot be "rebuilt" and remain the same forest, but we could probably rebuild a forest similar to the original if we knew how. No one has ever done it.

A major difference between automobiles, human bodies, and forests is that we designed and built automobiles, so we have parts catalogs, maintenance manuals, and can manufacture and substitute any part we wish. We have service departments to do all of this for us—at some cost. We also know a great deal about human bodies. We have a parts catalog, a maintenance manual, and a service department. Our bodily parts, such as blood, kidneys, etc., are somewhat interchangable between humans, and some parts can be manufactured—at some cost, but less efficiently than an automobile because we did not design and build our bodies and still have a great deal to learn.

A forest, on the other hand, is more complex, has more pieces and moving parts, and more processes that are hidden and unknown than either an automobile or a human body, and we can't ask it how it feels. Most critical, we do not have a parts catalog, or a maintenance manual, and we don't know which parts, if any, are substitutable. Further, we don't have a service department to rebuild a forest in any semblance of its original self if we could define what that was. And we do not know what the cost would be if we could do it. Because we can't repair a forest, the cost of its destruction is currently incalculable. We may not realize that we have crossed the final threshold until we have irreparably damaged the environment in which not just the forest but people must live.

It is easier to put a person on the moon than it is to manage one acre of forest. Putting a person on the moon is a process in black and white; you either hit it or miss it. But managing a forest acre is all gray. There are infinitely many more pieces and total unknowns in an acre of ground than in a spaceship. A forest is a billion-piece jigsaw puzzle, and most of the pieces are the same indistinguishable shade with edges that tend to shift and blur. No wonder we prefer to lift out and use the few pieces we recognize.

## On genetics and Swiss bank accounts

Genetic manipulation of forest trees was born in the concept of short-term economic expediency. By necessity, this process ignores long-term ecological ramifications to and within the forest as a whole, because tenable management practices for short-term profits must be based on predictable results. Some people think of "genetic improvements" as the panacea of forestry just as some people think of secret, numbered Swiss accounts as the panacea of banking. The only "panacea" in management of natural resources is an apparently unlimited supply of virgin resources, such as old-growth Douglas fir, but that is a gift from God that we are given only once per acre. We have spent and are spending both ours and the future's. Genetic manipulation is a human arrogance for which there are hidden costs analogous to those of Swiss bank accounts. In a very simplistic sense, three hidden costs can be shown for genetic manipulation of forest trees.

89

The first is lack of predictability in our unique forests of the Pacific Northwest; we can't predict any results because no one has yet grown a "genetically improved" forest for even one rotation—let alone two, three, or more. We are playing "genetic roulette" with future forests, a dangerous game about which more will be discussed later.

The second hidden cost is that, by manipulating the genetics of the trees, we are altering the function of ecological processes in the entire managed forest because we are changing how the individual trees function. For example, if they grow faster they will have larger cells and more sapwood—less heartwood—which changes the way they recycle in the soil (Maser et al. 1988b). That, in turn, alters all other connected biological functions. And we don't even know what these functions are, let alone what difference they will make in the long-term health of the forest.

The third hidden cost is demonstrated in Figure 14. An unmanaged forest (Fig. 14-A) is like a numbered Swiss bank

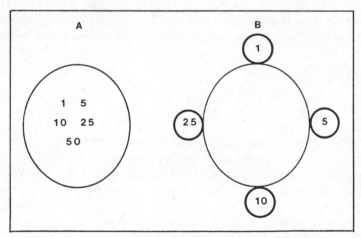

Fig. 14. An unmanaged forest has unlimited genetic variability, represented in A by enough denominations of coin to make exact change from any denomination of currency. Genetic specialization, B, has the hidden trade-off of giving up genetic flexibility in that the forest is no longer so adaptable to changes in climate, pollution, etc. What is gained in short-term, fast growth is gained at the expense of long-term ability of the forest to adapt to constantly changing environmental circumstances. We are therefore jeopardizing long-term biological health of the forest for short-term economic gains.

account that has a complete denomination of its own particular coin currency. The currency in the forest (called stored genetic variability) is unseen, as is the currency in the Swiss bank account. One does not have to see the currency in order to get the correct change. If there is an unlimited amount of money in the bank account, as there is genetic variability in the unmanaged forest, then you can get the exact change for any denomination you choose, even from an automatic, mechanical teller. To a forest, that means it can, within limits, adapt genetically to changes in climate from a human-caused greenhouse effect due to loss of atmospheric ozone, natural climatic changes, increasing air pollution, etc. When we withdraw genetic variability (currency) from the forest's genetic account (we remove the 10 in Fig. 14-A), we begin to artificially limit the forest's ability to adapt to changing conditions—something it must continually do to survive. Without the 10-cent coin you can no longer get the exact change from your Swiss bank account; you are now limited; you have lost flexibility as to what transactions you can make.

Now let's take this one step further. We cut down a forest across the landscape from northern Oregon to southern Oregon and from the Pacific coast to the crest of the western Cascade Mountains. We then plant Douglas fir seedlings "genetically improved" to grow quickly. In addition, seedlings planted in northern Oregon are selected to withstand cold, those in the south to withstand heat, those in the west to withstand wet weather, and those in the east to withstand dry weather and short growing seasons. In order to gain genetic selectivity, we have artifically adapted the trees to our set of values. When this is done, we give up flexibility—the tree's inherent ability to adapt to changing conditions. As an analogy, let's pretend you are travelling in Switzerland and that the central bank with your numbered account is in Geneva. Only the central bank has all denominations of currency (Fig. 14-A). As you travel in northern Switzerland, you find satellite, mechanical bank tellers from which you can make change, but they only have and give a denomination of 1, a penny (Fig. 14-B). In the east you find a teller that only has 5's, in the south only 10's, and in the west only 25's. The selected currency of the satellite tellers restricts your ability to adapt to unexpected business necessities; your loss of flexibility can cause considerable unforeseen hardship. It's the same with a forest. Nature allows for changes in climate and equips the trees with the genetic ability to adapt and survive. What happens when we rob the forest of its "excess genes" and then comes a wet weather cycle in our chosen "dry" forest?

Armed only with short-term economic projections based on rational, linear thinking, we are genetically "improving"—and biologically jeopardizing—our forests. And the allowable cut (not the amount of timber that may be cut but that which "shall" be cut) has been increased because of these projections. This is not a new phenomenon, however, because we tout modern forestry as agriculture, and in some ways it is:

> American agriculture has been powerfully persuasive in the world, even among those who profess to live by different principles. Its willingness to take risks for increased production has set a pace that other nations, such as the Soviet Union, feel constrained to follow—just as less aggressive plains farmers have been led to emulate their more affluent entrepreneurial neighbors. There may be many reasons why people misuse their land. But the American Dust Bowl of the thirties suggests that a capitalist-based society has a greater resource hunger than others, greater eagerness to take risks, and less capacity for restraint (Worster, 1979, p. 7).

There is a final point to bear in mind. Genetically "improved" trees represent a new, untested product (the first hidden cost), and American business has had much experience with new products. Consider the risk of new-product failure:

> The firm [forest industry], its customers [American public], and society at large [future generations] have an important stake in the efficient management of the innovation, new-product process. The firm's direct expenditure on research and development are large and must be judged by their ability to yield superior new products and processes. *During development, the market success of a new product is always in doubt* [emphasis mine]. In fact, a large proportion of all programs are terminated before achieving market success. . . . A number of industries indicated less than 15 percent of all development projects resulted in commercially successful products and that a full 37 percent of all products that reached the market proved to be commercial failures [such as weak wood from fast-grown coniferous trees (Senft et al. 1985)]. These rates varied only moderately across the major industries that were studied. . . . The seven most convincing studies placed the failure rate following market introduction at about 40 percent. . . . It should be emphasized, however, that the type of products examined, the period of time covered, and the definitions used can all have a pronounced effect on the reported failure [or success] rate (Pessemier 1982, pp. 8 and 9).

The products Pessemier discussed were all conceived, studied, designed, studied, manufactured, studied, and marketed by people for people, and still there is no guarantee of success. When we "redesign" trees we also redesign the entire functional forest—and how little we know about the consequences of that! A new product on the consumer market succeeds or fails in months. The success or failure of a redesigned forest will not become apparent for about a century. If we fail, then what? I think it prudent, therefore, to experiment with small acreages of genetically "improved" trees rather than committing thousands of acres to potential disaster by borrowing from the future and increasing the allowable cut based on assumptions—with no data and no collateral (Bella and Overton 1972).

## A forest is cyclic not linear

The main reason we treat forests as commodities is that our thinking, as earlier discussed, has become linear and rational. A forest, however, is neither linear nor rational (Fig. 15). It is cyclic and

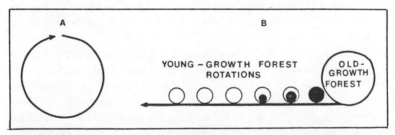

Fig. 15. There are two ways of viewing a forest: cyclic (A) or linear (B). There is no waste in a cyclic view because, by definition, everything is recycled somewhere in the system. We have, however, built economic waste into our linear view of a forest. Short-term economics decrees that anything not used by humans is a waste. Our view, short-term economic expediency, is that we can liquidate old-growth forests and forever harvest even-aged, rapidly growing young forests with a sustained yield (open circles). Reality—depicted by the solid circles—shows a decrease in productivity over time (Plochmann 1968, p. 24) because we are unbalancing the forests system by withdrawing capital without reinvestment, which impairs its ecological ability to function over time.

unpredictable. When we liquidate an old-growth forest, we do so thinking we can forever have a rapidly growing young forest that has a magic sustained yield, even as we ignore the four cornerstones of forestry—soil, water, air, and sunlight. If we were to

93

recalculate yield tables for a given acre after each rotation, I think we would find, as pointed out by Plochmann (1968), that it does not work the way we insist on thinking it does (Fig. 15). Yields are not sustainable until we first learn how to sustain the basis for these yields—healthy and productive forests. To my knowledge, no one has yet done this.

Sustain is defined as: to supply with sustenance, to keep up. Sustenance, in turn, means support or maintenance, nourishment, something that gives support, endurance, or strength. The question is, how is sustained yield defined? Are three crops of corn, at the same number of bushels per acre, considered a sustained yield by a farmer? Three crops of corn take only three years to produce. Three 80-year rotations of timber, at the same volume of woodfiber per acre, take 240 years to produce. If three crops of corn are not considered to be a sustainable crop because the yield drops and the soil is finally exhausted, why are three crops of trees considered to be sustainable forestry? The only difference is the length of time it takes to grow three crops—three years instead of 240 years, but it's still only three crops of corn and three crops of trees.

We have not practiced "sustainable-yield forestry" in the Pacific Northwest because our "sustained yield" has come from old-growth we inherited from Nature and for which we can claim no credit. As we propose to practice it, it is by and large short-term economic exploitation. We harvest the principal of soil-nutrient capital we inherited without reinvesting sufficient capital in the forest, either within or between rotations, to at least balance the account. We violate ecological principles of diversity, process interactions, and time in order to practice exploitive forestry, and then we anoint our diminishing return by the name "sustained yield."

Further, so far as I can determine, the way we propose to practice "sustainable-yield forestry" is exclusive of all other human values except production of fast-grown woodfiber. Young forests do not produce the highest quality water; they are not conducive to recreation; spotted owls are not sustained by them through time, nor are elk; and finally, they have lost the attractiveness of diversity that we, as humans, seek in our outdoor recreational-spiritual-rejuvenating experiences.

On top of all this, Senft and colleagues (1985, pp. 477 and 478) have shown that fast-grown trees make problem lumber because of weak wood that tends to shrink, warp, and break under stress (Fig. 15-B) (Photo 37):

Photo 37. Lumber made from weak, rapidly grown plantation wood. Note the warping and bending (arrows). (Photograph by Brian Egan.)

The housing industry has documented over 700 cases of a new and unpredictable phenomenon called the rising trus. . . . fast tree growth is increasing the percentage of juvenile wood in timber harvested from plantations in the South and West.

Plantation foresters herald new, "improved", "genetically engineered" trees as an answer to future timber shortages. They may be right, but advocates of "bigger and faster is better" face a two-sided problem: maintaining wood strength and dimensional stability while increasing stem diameter growth. [The problem is at least three-sided when depletion of soil fertility and impairment of ecological processes are added.] The race to produce maximum timber volume per acre cannot ignore consumers' needs for forest products best produced by slow growth (Harris 1981). Maximum volume, obtained by plantation culture or by silvicultural manipulation, may be fine for pulp and paper but not for studs. An underlying concern for forest managers must be product quality. Fast-grown, short-rotation conifers lack the woodfiber needed for products requiring structural strength. . . .

The impetus for plantations came initially from the desire of the pulp and paper industry to maximize fiber output from timberland. The result was a successful research effort to select, genetically screen, and silviculturally manage tree species to produce more volume per acre and shorten the harvest rotation time.

This was a logical [short-term economic] course of action for the paper industry. Even so, many pulp mills still prefer old-growth stems with narrower rings, higher density, higher pulp yields, and lower cost.

Maximum timber yield entails additional costs of regular thinning cuts and short rotations. Wood processed into pulp does not return the profit per unit of wood used for other purposes. Inevitably, wood cultured and managed for pulp is being processed for lumber.

## What you see is not the whole story

As noted before, the forest we see aboveground is, in large measure, a reflection of the soil's ability to grow that stand of trees. Let's take another look at this relationship. The original old-growth forest has three prominent characteristics: large live trees, large snags, and large fallen trees (Franklin et al. 1981). The large snags and large fallen trees become part of the forest floor and eventually are incorporated into the forest soil, where a myriad of organisms and processes make the nutrients stored in the decomposing wood available to the living trees. Furthermore, the changing habitats of the decomposing wood allow nitrogen fixation (the conversion of atmospheric nitrogen to a form usable by living trees) by free-living bacteria to take place (Harmon et al. 1986, Maser et al. 1987b). These processes are possible through Nature's "roll over" accounting system—the large dead trees are a reinvestment of forest capital into the growing forest (Fig. 16) (Photo 38).

The advent of intensive forestry disallowed this finely tuned practice, the reinvestment of forest capital (large dead wood) in future forests. In May 1985, I examined soil pits three to five feet deep in the intensively managed forests of southern Germany. There is no large woody debris in the soil of those forests nor has there been for well over a century, and productivity has been declining accordingly (Plochmann 1968). When the hardwood forest was first converted to softwood plantations, however, yield of woodfiber (first rotation of intensive forestry) (Fig. 16) was high, but then it declined steadily (Plochmann 1968). Are our forests following the same pattern because we practice intensive forestry with the same philosophical foundation as German foresters from whom we learned?

96

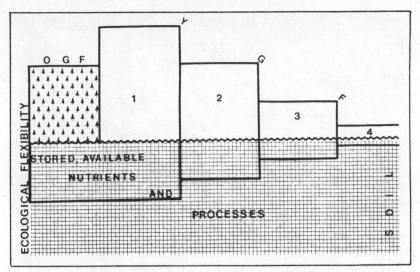

Fig. 16. The original old-growth forest (OGF) created much large woody debris (fallen trees) that became incorporated into the forest floor and soil. These fallen trees, with all their attendent organisms and processes, are a vital storehouse of available nutrients and nutrient cycles on which the living forest depends. Note that the first rotation (1) in the young-growth forest (YGF) produces more woodfiber per unit area per unit time than exists in the old-growth stand. But rotations 2, 3, and 4 decrease in the amount of woodfiber produced per unit area per unit time. Note that the amount of woody debris in the soil decreases also and, with intensive forestry, is not replaced; this translates into ecological brittleness as opposed to ecological flexibility.

The apparent success of the first rotation on which intensive short-rotation management is grounded is deceiving. The rest of the story lies belowground. There appears to be unlimited energy and intact processes for sustained high production of woodfiber when the stored available nutrients and processes from the liquidated old-growth forest are available for the first rotation (Maser et al. 1987b, Spies and Cline 1987). Without balancing withdrawals, investments, and reinvestments, however, both interest and principal are spent and productivity declines (Fig. 16).

Do not mistake planting seedlings (reforestation or aforestation) or fertilization as reinvestments; they patently are not reinvestments in the forest! Except for liquidating the inherited old-growth trees, planting seedlings on cutover acres and fertilizing the young stand is the *initial economic investment.* A forest does not run on

Photo 38. Large, fallen trees that decompose and recycle into the forest soil are a reinvestment of nutrient capital and ecological processes into the next forest. For example, a fallen tree oriented along the contour of a slope has the upslope side filled with humus and inorganic material that allows invertebrates and small vertebrates to tunnel alongside. The downslope side provides protective cover for larger vertebrates. The wood itself is saturated with water and acts as a reservoir under protection of the forest canopy. (USDA Forest Service photograph by J.F. Franklin.)

dollars; it runs on such things as decomposing wood—large fallen trees—that Nature reinvested in Her forest. As we redesign the forest, we will be wise to acknowledge Nature's blueprint. After all, She created the forest and only She understands the whole story.

## Ace is low

In cards, as most people know, the ace is to be coveted. It can, however, be high (follow the king) or be low (act as a one) as dictated by the game. In forestry, the ace is low—low elevation, easily accessible, highly productive, timber-growing sites. The most productive low-elevation forests (below 4,000 ft.) were the first to be cut out. To maintain the "sustained yield" from the less productive high-elevation forests (above 4,000 ft.), ". . . *the increase in annual acreage cut has been five times greater than the increase in volume cut during the last 40 years''* [emphasis mine] (Harris 1984). Are we adding to other ecological blunders of world forestry by mining our high-elevation watersheds? Let's consider again the Dust Bowl of the 1930's:

> The Dust Bowl was the darkest moment in the twentieth-century life of the southern plains. The name suggests a place—a region whose borders are as inexact and shifting as a sand dune. But it was also an event of national, even planetary, significance. A widely respected authority on world food problems, Georg Borgstrom, has ranked the creation of the Dust Bowl as one of the three worst ecological blunders in history. [I include tropical deforestation as the fourth global catastrophe.] The other two are the deforestation of China's uplands about 3,000 B.C., which produced centuries of silting and flooding, and the destruction of Mediterranean vegetation by livestock, which left once fertile lands eroded and impoverished. Unlike either of those events, however, *the Dust Bowl took only 50 years to accomplish* [emphasis mine]. It cannot be blamed on illiteracy or overpopulation or social disorder. It came about because the culture was operating in precisely the way it was supposed to. Americans blazed their way across a richly endowed continent with a ruthless, devastating efficiency unmatched by any people anywhere. When the white men came to the plains, they talked expansively of "busting" and "breaking" the land. And that is exactly what they did. Some environmental catastrophes are nature's work, others are the slowly accumulating effects of ignorance or poverty. *The Dust Bowl, in contrast, was the inevitable outcome of a culture that deliberately, self-consciously, set itself that task of dominating and exploiting the land for all it was worth* [emphasis mine] (Worster 1979, p. 4).

Because the industrialists' view of the land is conceived in profits (and they are absolutely right from their point of view), we need to understand money. Money has no value in and of itself. Money is symbolic of the value we place on something else, such as food, clothing, a home, an automobile, etc. In fact, money is defined as: something generally accepted as a medium of exchange—a go-between for things we value, a measure of value for something, or a means of payment for something we want. By the same token, the amount of money we are willing to reinvest in the forests to ensure their sustainability through time is a measure of the value we perceive in them. But money spent without humility—without honoring Nature's design—can still kill a forest.

99

To understand the impact of forest management for profit, we need to examine a forest that extends from sea level to timberline (Fig. 17). First we will take a look at the virgin forest (Fig. 17-A). Note that the amount of natural stress (column 2) is correlated with elevation (column 1); this means that the higher the elevation the shorter the growing season, the greater the temperature extremes, the poorer the soil, the greater the natural stress of survival for the forest—and vice versa at low elevations. If the virgin forest is now managed (Fig. 17-B), column three is introduced and management stress is added to the forest's endeavor to survive through time. The initial clearcutting of the old-growth timber puts a dispropor-tionate stress (management stress) on the forest that is correlated

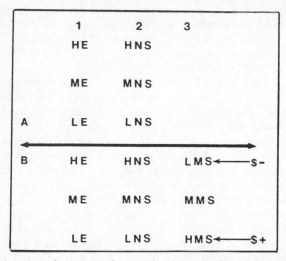

Fig. 17. A is a virgin forest going from sea level to timberline. Column 1 represents: high elevation (HE), mid elevation (ME), and low elevation (LE). Column 2 represents: high natural stress (HNS), moderate natural stress (MNS), and low natural stress (LNS). B is the same forest under management where column 3 represents: low management stress (LMS), moderate management stress (MMS), and high management stress (HMS). In an unmanaged forest (A) columns 1 and 2 are in balance and the forest is self-sustaining, self-repairing through time. In the managed forest (B) the addition of column 3 (forestry) disrupts the ecological balance. The high-elevation forest is the least inherently resilient and is where we have the greatest impact ecologically each time we log, yet this is where we spend the least dollars to care for the health of the system that produces the trees because this is where we perceived the smallest profit margin to be. Conversely, the low-elevation forest is the most inherently resilient and is therefore where we have the least impact ecologically each time we log, yet this is where we spend the most dollars to care for the health of the system that produces the trees because this is where we perceived the largest profit margin to be.

with columns one and two, natural stress and elevation (Harris 1984). Note where most of the money is spent (low elevation, low natural stress forest) and where the least money is spent (high elevation, high natural stress forest).

Low-elevation forests, with inherently low natural stress, are the most productive in terms of woodfiber; so these forests have the greatest potential to produce profits (Photo 39). Therefore, the vast

Photo 39. Low-elevation forests are highly productive of woodfiber and are ecologically resilient. (USDA Forest Service photograph.)

majority of the perceived value of the forest is here, so the vast majority of the money (Fig. 17-B) and the greatest intensity of management activity is centered in these low-elevation forests. Ironically, however, it is exactly this perceived value that causes an increase in money to be spent to change the forest—to "improve" Nature's design, fast and drastically, based almost entirely on predicted profit margins from short-term economics but without hard scientific data.

High-elevation forests, on the other hand, produce little woodfiber and produce it slowly (Photo 40). They therefore have little perceived value once they are cut, so little money is spent on them compared to low-elevation forests. But they already are near or at the limits of natural stress so any management activity is

Photo 40. High-elevation forests are marginally productive of woodfiber and are ecologically fragile. (USDA Forest Service photograph.)

disproportionately stressful (Fig. 17-B). There is, however, little profit to be made from high-elevation forests because they grow slowly and do not reach sufficient size to produce woodfiber at a high enough profit margin per dollar invested. Thus the perceived value of high-elevation forests has almost the exact opposite effect as the perceived value of low-elevation forests. Ironically here, however, the insensitivity with which we manage high-elevation forests—based on perceived profit margin from woodfiber produced for dollars spent—is likely to lower forest productivity fast and drastically, based almost entirely on predicted profit margins from short-term economics but without hard scientific data concerning the consequences of such management.

I have used elevation only as one example; the soils of southwestern Oregon are another. There are, in fact, forested areas that humility and wisdom dictate should not be cut even once, regardless of the perceived short-term dollar value of the woodfiber.

# Where are you?

We cannot be present if we are thinking either about the past or the future. *We are mentally where we think we are* (Fig. 18). The same is true in managing our forests.

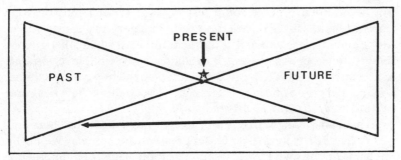

Fig. 18. If you want to be the star on stage in your life, you have to be present. If you are jetting from the past to the future or the future to the past, there is no one home—you're off stage. You can only be on stage—the star of your performance—when you're present in the theater.

Have you ever noticed, for example, that the present is seldom quite right, seldom seems to be good enough to natural resource industrial stockholders, economists, and managers. The past was "the good ol' days" with unlimited resources and few or no regulations controlling exploitation, and the future, the next planning cycle, the next stand of young trees, will be better. But now—the present—is not okay (Fig. 18). The point is: the forest industry, forest economists, and forest managers take past values, both in dollars per unit of raw materials and quantity of "renewable" raw materials produced per acre, and project them into the future—skipping the present (Fig. 18). The conservation-oriented public, on the other hand, wants things now—old-growth forests now, spotted owls now, clean water now, elk now—not yesterday, not tomorrow, *now.*

Keep in mind that the present, the here and now, is all we have; *this is it, folks!* Yesterday is past and gone, we can't change it—opportunities lost are lost. Tomorrow is not here and we have no idea, despite our aspirations, hopes, and expectations, what it will bring. In reality, "tomorrow" is something that is always coming but never comes. Scarlett O'Hara's motto was, "I'll think about that tomorrow," and her life added up to "Gone with the Wind." The present, the here and now, is all we have; it's all we will ever have. *This is it, folks!*

Have you ever had someone interrupt your thoughts and ask, "Where are you?" And you say, "I'm sorry; I was thinking." "About what?" "Well, I'm going to Hawaii next month, and I was just thinking about the trip." One could just as easily knock gently on your forehead and ask, "Are you in there?" In a very real sense, you're not home. Unless you are in there, at home, it's like talking to an empty house, or as some say, "I'm talking to myself!" Have you ever driven from point A to point B and not realized how you got there? Again, there is no one home; there is a robot behind the wheel, and it's a dangerous way to drive.

What I am saying is that few of us are "present" in the "here and now" (Fig. 18). Note the star under present. The only way we can be an actor in our own play is to be *present* on stage at all times—not constantly jetting between the past and the future (Fig. 18). Perhaps one of the greatest challenges we face each day is that of being present, of being "home" in our bodies now so that when you talk to me I am there. My wife Zane still asks me, "Are you in there?" And then says, when I have returned from my mental travels, "I rang your bell and no one was home."

To be *present*, in the sense of being *mentally here, now* is a difficult concept to define because there really is no word that means mental presence as opposed to simple physical presence. So, let's examine what it means not to be present. You are thinking about (remembering) the past, let's say last year's vacation, which was your first trip to Hawaii. You flew to Hawaii and had a very rough trip. You are afraid of flying anyhow, so the unexpected, "unseasonal" storm really frightened you, but once in Hawaii, you had a marvelous time. Because you are flying to Hawaii next month for your long-anticipated vacation, you begin to think more and more about how much fun you had last year and that you expect this year to be even better. Suddenly, out of "nowhere," you vividly remember last year's flight and you become afraid that next month's flight might be the same. In all of your reverie, you are either in the *past* or in the *future,* and now you are jerked into the present as your car sputters and you coast to the side of the road out of gas. "Damn! I was so busy thinking, I missed the gas station!"

When the forest industry, forest economists, and forest managers carry one step further the projection of the past to the future (Fig. 18), they assume that the future young-growth forest will produce as much or more woodfiber per acre as the original old-growth forest (Fig. 19-A). That assumption is based on four premises, all

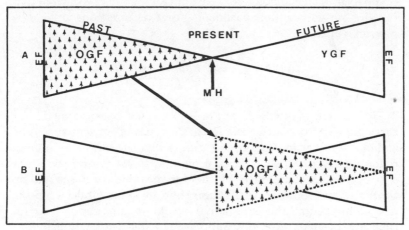

Fig. 19. The forest industry, forest economists, and forest managers perceive a "magic hinge" (MH in A) (scientific research and technology) in the present that will make the young-growth forest (YGF) "better" than the old-growth forest (OGF). The concept is that future forests can be made sustainable, with the same ecological functions (EF), on a short-rotation basis. This notion is based on experience with the old-growth forest that is economically projected to the young-growth forest (A). Experience in liquidating an old-growth forest is past tense, however, and has little or nothing to do with data on how to redesign and grow a new sustainable, short-rotation forest even when projected into the future (B).

false: The first is that each acre can and will grow at least the volume of woodfiber that was represented in the harvested old-growth stand. The second is that the first premise is true because soil fertility, water quality and quantity, air quality, and sunlight quality are constants. The third is that young-growth forests function the same as old-growth forests, only faster and better. And the fourth is that a "magic hinge" exists in the present (scientific research and technology) that will make the future forest more productive of woodfiber than the past forest—or at least a mirror reflection of the past forest in yield (Fig. 19-A).

All these false premises are based on experience with old-growth, not data with young-growth, and old-growth experience tells us nothing about either the ecological functions (processes) or the sustainability of short-rotation, young-growth forests (Fig. 19-B). In short, the concept of short-rotation forestry is an economic concept and has nothing to do with biology of forests (Hummel 1985). As noted earlier, economic short-rotations arose in Germany and have not worked as expected (Plochmann 1968) (Fig. 15). Some form of sustainable short-rotation forestry may work, but that remains an assumption based on other assumptions until it is proven, which no one has done!

## Planning—our half-used data

This section is subtitled "our half-used data" because we do not carry our planning out far enough to show us the consequences our actions have set in motion. Put differently, short-term economic planning discloses short-term economic forestry, and does not show what the cumulative effects of management actions will be through time. So, we leave the future blindly to the future. True, we cannot foresee all the cumulative effects of our actions through time, and perhaps we really cannot wait to know everything before we do anything. But there definitely are some effects we can project, based on data we do have. Instead we stubbornly persist in ignoring these data.

One of the problems we face is that forests are long lived, especially those of the Pacific Northwest, so a forester sees a rotation-age stand on a given acre precisely once in her or his career—even if it's a very short 40-year rotation (Fig. 20). The first career forester works with the original old-growth stand (cuts it and replants the area) but has no historical knowledge of the stand and cannot foresee what will happen to the future stand, despite all the assumptions, predictions, and data. Career forester two sees the first rotation forest at harvest time. Career forester three will be the person involved in harvesting the second short-rotation, and career forester four the third short-rotation forest. That means that every career forester would see a managed stand on a given acre only once at harvest time. The forester may or may not have good historical data on the stand and cannot foresee the future of the stand.

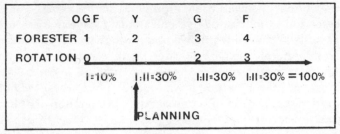

Fig. 20. Because of the longevity of Pacific Northwest forests, a career forester only sees a stand or rotation once at harvest on any acre, be it old-growth (OGF) or young-growth (YGF). Let's assume that 10 percent of the potential recycleable nutrients will be removed with the woodfiber taken out at each entry. Each time a human enters the forest to manipulate it in a way that removes woodfiber (l in the figure is equal to an individual entry), 10 percent of the potential recycleable nutrients will be removed. So, harvest entry into the old-growth forest represents a 10 percent removal (l=10%), as does each entry in plantation management that removes woodfiber, such as site preparation and planting (l=10%), commercial thinning (l=10%), and final harvest (l=10%). In precommercial thinning, represented by the colon (:), no nutrients are removed from the site and so the colon is equal to zero. Thus removal of woodfiber is additive over time: old-growth (l=10%) + first rotation (l=10% + :=0 +1=10% + 1=10%, which adds up to 30 percent per rotation) + second rotation (30%) + third rotation (30%) all adds up to 100 percent removal of the potential recycleable nutrients. Thus, the soil would be exhausted by the end of the third short-rotation. We, however, plan only for the next entry, the next 10 years, so we neither know, see, understand, nor are accountable for the cumulative effects caused by our actions.

Now, I'm going to select a figure—*without any scientific data*—that is easy to compute, say 10 percent of the potential recyclable nutrients (Fig. 20). I'm also going to assume that whatever woodfiber (product) is removed from an acre of forest during harvest of old-growth and subsequent site preparation and planting, commercial thinning, and final harvest will remove 10 percent of the potential recyclable nutrients (fertility) that would have remained and been recycled into the next stand had they not been removed with the woodfiber (Fig. 20). As can be seen (Fig. 20), if we were to account for each 10 percent removal of nutrients, we would deplete soil nutrients by the end of the third short-rotation forest, and career forester five probably would not even know what happened or why. We do not plan far ahead; we plan only for the next entry, the next 10-year cycle (Fig. 20). We do not plan for even three short 80-year rotations (three crops of trees) that would take 240 years to grow. It is, of course, not this simple

107

because there are some nutrient inputs and disruption of ecological processes and other cumulative effects that I have not accounted for. Nevertheless, what would we find through time if we looked at fertilizers, *or* herbicides, *or* pesticides, *or* soil compaction, *or* alteration of drainage patterns, *or* forest fragmentation, *or, or . . . ?* What would we find through time if we looked at fertilizers, *and* herbicides, *and* pesticides, *and* soil compaction, *and* alteration of drainage patterns, *and* forest fragmentation, *and, and . . . ?*

Is our lack of foresight, *our emphasis on economic rotations rather than biological rotations,* part of the worldwide forest decline? Is this what Plochmann (1968) was beginning to understand and trying to tell us about German forests? I don't know, but I am convinced that we are ignoring the most important aspect of our existing data in forest land-use planning—the forecasting of the possible ecological consequences that could stem from economically oriented actions over three or more short rotations. As I have said before, we face grave, uncomfortable uncertainties in our renewable resource management decisions, or for that matter in all land-use decisions, because we are giving economics and technology higher priority than we are according scientific understanding (Fig. 10).

## Part Three

## CHANGE, WHY ARE WE AFRAID OF IT?

*The unleashed power of the atom has changed
everything save the way we think and thus we drift
toward unparalleled catastrophe.*
> —Albert Einstein

As we move toward a new design for forests, we need to pause and consider the whole matter of changes. Large changes are indeed called for, and they are not merely a matter of trees. Change is defined as: to make different in some way. Change is definable mainly in terms of its opposite, constancy—that which is constant. Long-term changes, such as occur in unmanaged forests, are seen by short-lived human beings as constants. Constant is defined as: something that is invariable or unchanging. If everything were constant, change would not exist. We are comfortable with that which appears to be constant because it lulls us into thinking that we know what to expect. We take constancy for granted, however, and are surprised, often hurt, and sometimes terrified when we find that change has occurred. We therefore do our best to avoid change in ways that we are not even aware of. According to Bella (1987a), organizations, such as the U.S. Forest Service and the Bureau of Land Management, launder data and information for the "good" of the respective agency but not with the intent of dishonesty or malice. And I agree. Bella (p. 360) states:

> Modern society depends... [on] organizational systems for much of its information, particularly with respect to the assessment of large-scale technological projects [such as management of our forests]. It is reasoned that organizations tend to distort information to meet organizational needs. Such distortions do not depend upon dishonest behavior on the part of individuals. Rather, tendencies to distort information are systemic properties of the organizational systems themselves. As the power of modern technology grows, the consequences of distorted assessments become more serious and potentially catastrophic. . . .

111

Change is inevitable, however, and we can learn something about change from Buddhism, the whole philosophy of which is based on the *acceptance of change*. The Buddha taught the Four Noble Truths. The First Noble Truth—Truth of Suffering—states that the outstanding characteristic of the human situation is suffering or frustration, which comes from our difficulty in accepting that everything around us is impermanent and transitory. "All things," said the Buddha, "arise and pass away." The root of Buddhism is that flow and change are the basic features of Nature, and suffering arises whenever we resist the flow of life, whenever we try to control circumstances and cling to fixed forms, such as things, events, people, or ideas (Bukkyo Dendo Kyokai 1985, Capra 1975).

The second Noble Truth—Truth of the Cause of Suffering—deals with clinging or grasping. It is futile to grasp life from a wrong point of view, from ignorance. We divide the world we perceive into individual and separate things out of ignorance and thus attempt to confine fluid forms of reality in unchanging mental boxes. So long as we do this, we are bound to experience one frustration after another. Trying to create anything fixed or permanent in life and then trying to cling to its perceived permanence is a vicious circle, which is driven by karma, the never-ending chain of cause and effect (Bukkyo Dendo Kyokai 1985, Capra 1975) (see Fig. 1). As stated by the Buddha, "It is the everlasting and unchanging rule of this world that everything is created by a series of causes and conditions and everything disappears by the same rule; everything changes, nothing remains constant" (Bukkyo Dendo Kyokai 1985, p. 42).

This idea, that everything is constantly changing, that nothing is permanent, can be looked at another way—*acceptance of what is*. What is, is. It cannot be otherwise. I can't, for example, control circumstances, but I can control how I *react* to circumstances. If I simply accept the circumstance, I am in control of myself; if I fight the circumstance, try to control it, it controls me. What we resist persists.

One fascinating way in which people resist political and social change is to project their biases onto Nature. Taylor (1986, p. 334) cites a couple of interesting examples:

> . . . in the seventeenth century . . . during the English Civil War[,] the beehive, with its queen, drones or "nobles," and its workers, was regularly employed by Stuart supporters to defend

the concept of feudalism and social hierarchy. This tendency to project human values onto nature and then use such values to lend support to a particular world-view or social structure can again be witnessed throughout the nineteenth and twentieth centuries. Thus, for . . . William Bateson, the natural hierarchy of the biological world was seen to legitimize British class structure. Indeed, for a number of late nineteenth and early twentieth century thinkers, such concepts as biological hierarchy and homeostasis [a state of physiological equilibrium] were employed to validate and support those traditional values that were being eroded away in a rapidly expanding industrial world.

Acceptance of a circumstance—that which is—is based on the notion that you can't move away from a negative; you can only move towards a positive. To illustrate, you are near timberline on a mountain that is rich in patches of huckleberries. It is a warm, sunny, autumn afternoon and you are peacefully picking berries, sweet, juicy huckleberries. Suddenly you come face to face with a large bear also eating berries. Without thinking, you start to run away from the bear, and because you are running away from it, looking at the bear over your shoulder to see how close it is, you will either run into the tree you wanted to climb or you will run past it. Your other choice is to run toward the tree, not away from the bear. In this case, you focus all your attention on the tree and simply run like hell. You don't know where the bear is and you don't care, but you know exactly where the tree is and you care about that very much.

Go back to the discussion of "Where are you?" and reread it. You can only accept what is if you are present in the here and now. We, in Western culture, spend an inordinate amount of time wanting things, circumstances, to be different; we therefore frustrate ourselves by refusing to accept what is as it is now, right now, this instant. We cannot control circumstances, be they how a forest functions or how the market for woodfiber products acts over time. *We can only accept what is and control how we react to it* (Fig. 21a, b, c).

Because nothing is fixed or constant, no matter how much we insist on thinking it is, nothing is as it appears to be. As Capra (1975, p. 44) wrote, "Whenever the Eastern mystics express their knowledge in words—be it with the help of myths, symbols, poetic images or paradoxical statements—they are well aware of the limitations imposed by language and 'linear' thinking. Modern physics has come to take exactly the same attitude with regard to its verbal models and theories. They, too, are only approximate and necessarily inaccurate." The same is true in managing forests; everything we do is "only approximate and necessarily inaccurate." There are no absolutes.

So how do we deal with change? Taylor (1986) made an astute observation in regard to this question. He wrote (p. 334):

> Throughout Western literature, our descriptions of the natural world have reflected the values and biases of a given period in our history. Indeed, our perceptions of nature often tell us less about what is actually "out there" in the landscape, and more about the types of mental topography and projections that we carry about in our heads. It is natural, therefore that as values change, so too do our views regarding nature. . . .
>
> . . . the form that our Western knowledge has taken has been predicted . . . [on] . . . the "objectification" and control of other people as well as the natural environment. However, we are at a stage in history when—if only for our very survival—it becomes increasingly necessary to realize that our ultimate security lies not in the ongoing separation of ourselves from one another and the environment, and not in a consciousness based upon fragmentation and manipulation—but rather in the relinquishment of such thought patterns in favor of a consciousness of wholeness and integration. . . . And so in order to step successfully into the future, we must find the courage to step first into the deepest recesses of ourselves. . . .

Gentle reader, we cannot change history, and we cannot change each other. We can only change ourselves, and as we change ourselves, our perception of each other and everything else changes.

## No "enemies" are "out there"

Enemy is defined as: one seeking to injure, overthrow, or confound an opponent; something harmful or deadly; a hostile unit or force. Fear is defined as: an unpleasant, often strong emotion caused by anticipation or awareness of danger; reason for alarm. Frightened is defined as: to make afraid, terrify; to drive or force by frightening. There are no "enemies" "out there," only other frightened people who perceive the need to defend themselves from potential loss of what they value—dignity, a human resource that is strangely affected by the supply and demand for products from natural resources. We do not think of ourselves as an enemy

Fig. 21. (A) Everything is cyclic in Chinese thought; this notion is expressed in a symmetric arrangement of the dark *yin* and the bright *yang*. The rotational symmetry forcefully suggests a continuous cyclic movement: As the *yang* returns cyclically to its beginning, the *yin*, attaining its maximum, gives place to the *yang*. The two dots symbolize the idea that each time one of the forces, *yin* or *yang*, reaches its extreme, there already is contained within it the seed of its opposite.

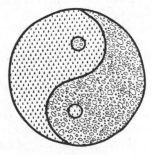

Fig. 21. (B) In this figure are the aboveground portion of the forest (tree crowns) and the belowground portion of the forest (tree roots and soil) shown in a dynamic cycle. The dots represent that old-growth forests recycle nutrients into the soil and the soil in turn gives up the nutrients to the next forest.

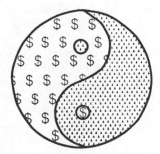

Fig. 21. (C) This figure represents the managed forest with forest biology and forest economics in a dynamic cycle. The dots represent the idea that a healthy forest is the most economical and it takes a reinvestment of mineral and organic capital in the forest to ensure its health.

because we are convinced that *our* position, *our* values are the *right* ones, and everyone knows "the enemy" is wrong. That is what we are taught. That is the unchanging, eternal verity around which Nationalism and Patriotism rally.

Stoessinger (1974) uncovered some enlightening common denominators in his book *Why Nations Go to War*. Some of his ideas (selected from pp. 219–230) are worth repeating here because when and where we see another human being as an enemy we perceive a potential war:

> 1. Turning to the outbreak of war, the case studies indicate the crucial importance of the personalities of leaders.
>
> 2. The . . . most important single precipitating factor in the outbreak of war is misperception. Such distortion may manifest itself in four different ways: in a leader's image of himself; a leader's view of his adversary's character; a leader's view of his adversary's intentions toward himself; and, finally, a leader's view of his adversary's capabilities and power.
>
> 3. Distorted views of the adversary's character also help to precipitate a conflict.
>
> 4. If a leader on the brink of war believes that his adversary will attack him, the chances of war are fairly high. If both leaders share this perception about each other's intent, war becomes a virtual certainty.
>
> 5. A leader's misperception of his adversary's power is perhaps the quintessential cause of war. It is vital to remember, however, that it is not the actual distribution of power that precipitates a war; it is the way in which a leader *thinks* that power is distributed.
>
> 6. Thus, on the eve of each war, at least one nation misperceives another's power. In that sense, the beginning of each war is a misperception or an accident. The war itself then slowly, and in agony, teaches men about reality.
>
> 7. At the very moment when mankind has the power to destroy the earth, men also have begun to perceive the planet as a whole.
>
> 8. Similarly, problems of resources and environment will be surmounted on a global basis or not at all. Thus, in both cases, the brute logic of the insensate machine has dictated a modicum of world order: the terror of atomic fire, and the prospect of man choking in his own waste. And out of this terror has sprung the recognition of the need for flexibility and change. The bomb must not become the earth, nor must the earth become the bomb.

What Stoessinger has outlined as war is a cycle of attack and defense based on the *judgment of appearances.* Appearance is defined as: outward aspect; outward indication, and judgment is defined as: the process of forming an opinion or evaluation by discerning and comparing; a proposition stating something believed or asserted; a formal utterance of an authoritative opinion. Our judgments are necessarily wrong because nothing is as it appears since appearance is external. Therefore, those whom we define as enemies are those whom we mistakenly perceive as dangerous. And mistake means to make a wrong judgment of character or ability based on inadequate knowledge. If we are not each other's enemies, what is the enemy? What are we afraid of? —change, loss of something we value through circumstances we cannot control.

Control, a synonym for power, is an interesting phenomenon in our lives. We pay dearly for control, but regardless of the price, there are limitations. For example, have you ever had a "bad" day, a day when nothing went right, a day when you "felt out of sorts"? On such a day, every little external thing that can go awry does so and unduly annoys you. That is because you "feel out of sorts," not at peace with yourself internally, and you therefore feel compelled to control the environment around you. If, on the other hand, you have a "good" day, a day when everything goes right, a day when you "feel in tune with the world," you have inner peace, inner control. On such a day, external things that still "delight" in going awry do not bother you. We cannot control circumstances. We can control how we react to circumstances, and that is both our problem and our solution. Because we are afraid of change, of loss, we want to remain the same and control the circumstances so other people— our perceived enemies—will have to risk change, but not us. There are no enemies out there, only people frightened of change, of being out of control, and therefore mistakenly rejected by their fellow human beings.

How does this relate to management of our forests? When we focus our attention on the human enemies we perceive in land-management agencies and industry, we are really focusing on the wrong thing, as Bella (1987a, p. 367–368) points out:

> ... Organizational systems filter information ... to protect their members from information unfavorable to the system itself and its behaviors. Organizational systems shape the perceptions and

117

beliefs of those within the organizations in ways that "keep the system going" even when catastrophic outcomes are involved.

The human fault that leads to the distortion of information is not limited to willful deceit. Individual honesty is necessary but insufficient to prevent the widespread distortion of information. The human fault of concern is more insidious than willful deceit. This fault involves the acceptance of a life that involves completing one's assignments. This hardly sounds untrustworthy, much less dangerous, but it is this "functionary" behavior that allows systematic distortions to occur.

Bella (1987a) goes on to say that a person who limits his or her inquiries and questions only to his or her assignments turns his or her mind over to the system and allows the "system" to shape it according to its needs. "One becomes a functionary of the system not by compromising one's beliefs, but rather, by turning responsibility for one's perceptions and beliefs over to the system." The fault lies not in the assignment but in not accepting personal responsibility for the outcome of the assignment on the environment and on society as a whole. Performing an assignment (simply taking orders without thinking about them ) is personally safe and environmentally and socially risky. On the other hand, it is often personally risky—if you want to keep your job—to question orders, which is what people in land-management agencies and industry are given, but to question the orders is both environmentally and socially responsible (Bella 1987b).

The point is that most professionals in land-management agencies and in industry are told what level of professionalism they will practice if they want to keep their jobs. So they trade their dignity and professionalism in on fear and that is what we judge them for. There are no enemies out there, only frightened people who have lost control of their lives to an ever-growing system that dehumanizes individuals in order to maintain itself.

## The crack in the sidewalk

Have you ever been dressed up in your Sunday finest and gone for a casual stroll on a warm, sunny afternoon? And as you saunter along feeling quite debonair you suddenly trip on a crack in the sidewalk. Instantly embarrassed and feeling foolish, you look around to see who saw you trip, who saw the "real" you. Feeling

118

foolish is one of our greatest fears because we think it leads to rejection by other people when they find out what we are "really" like.

Although "feeling foolish" seems to be one of our greatest fears, it is really only "performance anxiety." Performance anxiety is the fear of ridicule, rejection by other people as not being okay because they did not approve of our performance. Again, if someone actually laughs because you tripped on the crack, the person who laughed is judging appearances—a mistake—because by profession you are a tightrope walker who performs 50 feet above the ground with no net under you, and last Friday at the circus the person who just laughed applauded your performance as part of a standing ovation. The problem now is that the person who laughed simply did not recognize you. There was nothing personal in the laugh, but *you took it personally—and that is your choice.*

Even animals feel "foolish" and get "embarrassed." Have you ever watched a cat get embarrassed and sniff a table leg? It's really very common and is called "displacement activity." The cat is trying to shift attention from the "embarrassment" to the table leg. I used to have a small dog, Jamuna, who was fiercely protective—in her mind anyhow. We lived at the edge of a forest. I came home at dusk one evening, and as I walked up the gravel road, my little dog came roaring out snarling and barking at the top of her voice. She was in fact running right at me with great presence of mind because, when I spoke to her, she swerved just enough to race past me and give the unseen boogie behind me a good, professional barking. Then she came to greet me, "knowing" all the time that it was I.

Our fear of rejection by other people, of being judged as not okay, causes us to do a variety of things based on our perceived "need" to "protect ourselves from attack." Our major defense against attack is to become inaccessible (unknowable, a proverbial mystery). We become inaccessible in a number of ways. I used to be inaccessible by growing a large, bushy beard to so terrorize the world that people would keep their distance. When asked, "Why do you have a beard?" I would answer, "Anything that *hides* (to become inaccessible) the lower half of my face is an improvement." (The only problem was that I am bald and all that bush made me look like my head was on upside down!) My beard had become my identity. My dreams told me that. I used to dream that I was shaping my beard with a razor and, slipping, would cut a chunk out of it. I would then go into a blind panic because I was exposed—my "cover was blown."

119

Although I initially grew my beard as a creative gesture, it unconsciously became my identity and then my hiding place, my inaccessible retreat, my self-prison. We also hide behind mustaches, those little caterpillars that cling desperately to the upper lip and cringe every time the razor comes by. We hide behind dark glasses, big glasses, and glasses with fancy frames. Exuberancy with bright facial makeup is another way to hide. I used to have a neighbor who had to "put on her face" before she could face the day. I say hide because anything that diverts your eyes from contacting mine allows me to hide. After all, "the eyes are the window to the soul." We're really not different from a child standing in the middle of a bare room, covering his eyes with his hands and thinking he is hidden. The ultimate in being inaccessible these days—tuning out the world—is a fancy hat, dark glasses, a big beard, and earphones from which you can hear "music" emanating 10 feet away. And I do all this because I am afraid of you; afraid my performance of just being human is not up to your standard of what is "okay." Of course, since I'm also afraid to ask you what you think of me, I'll never know; I am afraid of not knowing, so I expect the worst and feel compelled to hide—to be inaccessible. And, in addition to all of this, we hide behind our social masks or persona, that carefully rehearsed and projected behavioral pattern that we think is acceptable to others while "hiding our real selves."

Again, what does this have to do with managing our forests? Well, if I feel trapped in an agency or industry that demands something less than my best professionalism, I am afraid of being not okay in your eyes, of being judged and found guilty because I am afraid to risk being honest with myself, which means I might have to resign to maintain my integrity. My job is at stake, and I'm afraid to resign because I don't know what I would do, and I don't feel good about my fear, so I hide behind my defensive masks. That way, I'm okay so long as you don't "know" me and find out how frightened I really am and how lousy I feel about my lack of courage. I'm okay so long as you don't challenge my professionalism—my ultimate mask—which brings up my self-failure, which I must then defend knowing all the time that I'm not being honest. Fear of being judged a nonprofessional becomes the crack in my sidewalk.

# To judge or not to judge

I always do the best I know how because my survival depends on it. Some days I may do something better than other days, yet each day is my best. My best is always tempered by how I feel, physically, mentally, and emotionally. You cannot see this, and I often do not know it; refresh your memory with our discussion about "good days" and "bad days." Of course, there is no such thing as a "good day" or a "bad day," there are only days in which our best is controlled by how we feel, not by what we think. When I tell myself that I "should" do better, I am anticipating what so and so would think if they only knew. I judge myself guilty for not living up to what I think so and so's expectations of me are. I don't ask them so I really don't know what they expect, but I still take myself to the mental woodshed and severely beat myself about the head and shoulders with a club named "guilt."

I believe *everyone*—everyone—does the level best he or she knows how to do at all times, myself included. If this is true, where is the basis for judgment? As stated in *A Course in Miracles* (Manual For Teachers 1975, p. 26):

> Judgment, like other devices by which the world of illusions is maintained, is totally misunderstood by the world. It is actually confused with wisdom, and substitutes for truth. As the world uses the term, an individual is capable of "good" and "bad" judgment, and his education aims at strengthening the former and minimizing the latter. There is, however, considerable confusion about what these categories mean. What is "good" judgment to one is "bad" judgment to another. Further, even the same person classified the same action as showing "good" judgment at one time and "bad" judgment at another time. Nor can any consistent criteria for determining what these categories are be really taught. At any time the student may disagree with what his would-be teacher says about them, and the teacher himself may well be inconsistent in what he believes. "Good" judgment, in these terms, does not mean anything. No more does "bad."
>
> It is necessary for the teacher of God to realize, not that he should not judge, but that he cannot. In giving up judgment, he is merely giving up what he did not have. He has actually merely become more honest. Recognizing that judgment was always impossible for him, he no longer attempts it.

I recently was on a TV program that I was told would air the issue of ancient forests from several points of view. The purpose of the program, I was led to believe, was to help the public understand the scope of the issue. In reality, however, the program was staged as a battlefield on which the moderator both directed and fueled the fires of war at the enormous cost of human dignity. And as the battle raged all around me, I could hear nothing but the drums of fear.

Fear, as I mentioned, is defined as a feeling of alarm or disquiet caused by the expectation of danger, pain, or disaster; a state or condition of alarm or dread. The definition of fear reminds me of a little dog I once knew named "Buster." Buster was afraid of the dark for some unknown but very important reason, important to Buster at least. Every night before Buster was put to bed in the utility room, he had to go outside. That meant Buster must face his fear—the dark out-of-doors—every night, and to bolster his courage, every night he played the same tune on his drum of fear. When Buster heard "bedtime," he flew into a frenzy of barking at the front door. When the door was opened, he dashed outside, hiked his leg on the nearest object, and raced back in, all the time barking at top decibel. Whether Buster's barking was to frighten boogies or to create so much noise that he did not have to listen to those awful night sounds, such as an owl hooting, or frogs croaking, or crickets chirruping, I don't know. All I do know is that every night Buster traded his dignity for fear and beat his drum for all it was worth.

As I again think about the TV program, the ancient forest comes to mind and with it a lesson in humility. When we look at an ancient forest, we focus on the large, old trees that to us signify primeval majesty, a deep sense of place, and a connectedness with ourselves in the past, the present, and the future, where for an instant time becomes irrelevant and forever is now.

Although there is something mystical about each old tree, only together can they give us our own, inner definition of an ancient forest. And yet, we do not even see the forest for the trees. Could we but see belowground, we would find gossamer threads from special fungi stretching for millions of miles through the soil. As described in Part I, special fungi grow on and in the feeder roots of the ancient trees as symbionts that not only acquire food, in the form of plant sugars, from the ancient trees' roots but also provide soil nutrients, vitamins, and growth regulators to the ancient trees. These symbiotic fungus-root structures (mycorrhizae) are the termini of the gossamer threads that form a complex fungal net under the entire ancient forest and, evidence suggests, connects all trees one to another.

The ancient forest over which the battle raged in the TV studio was unfortunately seen as a commodity of time, a pawn in a struggle of values, but not as a living organism. As the hour aged, the ancient forest became more and more of an isolated abstraction pierced by economic arrows and sliced by preservationist swords. And the protagonists, manipulated by the moderator, judged each other enemies. Thus, we too, the audience, became isolated abstractions. We became "The Forest Service," "The Conservationists," "The Industry," and we ceased to be human beings. We ceased to be human beings when we traded in our dignity on positions of defense and began to beat our drums of fear with all our strength.

What are we all so afraid of that we judge each other so harshly and condemn each other as enemies? We are all afraid of losing that which we value. Industrialists may fear the loss of the greatest profit margin they will ever have in forests—ancient trees that cost them nothing to grow, quality woodfiber that is essentially free for the taking, which if not taken is seen only as an economic waste. Conservationists may fear the loss of the same ancient trees because once gone, so are all other options that involve those trees. And most of the professionals in the public land management agencies are told, through insidious, covert, political pressure, what level of professionalism they will practice if they want to keep their jobs; and because they may be afraid of losing their jobs if they are honest in how they feel about what they are being told to do, they're damned if they do and damned if they don't.

We, like the ancient trees, appear as separate individuals, and we, like the ancient forest united by its belowground fungi, are united by our humanity. But we forget that we are human beings first and everything else second; so we blind ourselves to the fact that there are no "enemies" "out there," only other frightened people who perceive the need to defend themselves from potential loss of what they value—dignity. Dignity is a human resource that is strangely affected by the supply and demand for products from natural resources, and perceived scarcity often erodes human dignity. Of course, we are not the enemy, because our position is the right one, and everyone knows "the enemy" is wrong. The question is: by whose judgment is the "enemy" the enemy and by whose judgment is the enemy wrong? Now and always we must remember that is the time for mercy for as Gandhi pointed out, "An eye for an eye only makes the whole world blind."

We are products of our decisions, not victims of life. We make hundreds of decisions every day and each fits Robert Frost's poem "The Road Not Taken" (Lathem 1969, p. 105).

> Two roads diverged in a wood, and I—
> I took the one less traveled by,
> And that has made all the difference.

Each decision is a fork in our road of life; each fork is an option, an alternative, a choice. The direction of our lives is a result of many little decisions; a few we remember; most we don't. We usually remember the "big decisions," but we seldom realize that a single, big decision is merely a collection of little decisions along the way.

The life cycle of a salmon epitomizes the destination of choice. A long time ago, before Columbus sailed, a reddish orange egg was deposited in a redd (the gravelly stream bottom that serves as a "nursery" for salmon) in the headwaters of a Pacific Coast stream. There the egg lay for a time as Salmolétte developed inside. In time, Salmolétte hatched from the egg and struggled out of the gravel into the open water of protected places in the stream. There she grew until it was time to leave the stream of her beginning and venture into life. She could go only one way—downstream from small to larger and larger streams and rivers until at last she met the ocean. After some years at sea, the inner urge of her species drives Salmolétte, now an adult, along the Pacific Coast to find the precise river she had descended years earlier. Salmolétte must make a critical decision. If she selects the wrong river she will not reach her destination, regardless of all the other choices she makes. If Salmolétte swims into the exact river she had descended, she is on the right track, until she comes to the first fork and must choose again. Each time Salmolétte comes to a fork in the river, then large stream, then smaller stream, she must choose one or the other; she must accept what the chosen fork has to offer and forgo the possibilities of the fork not taken. Salmolétte can only return to the redd where her parents had deposited her as an egg if she knows where she is going and when she has arrived. Salmolétte's goal is to reach a particular place in a particular stream within a particular time to deposit her eggs to be fertilized by a male of her species. Salmolétte and her mate will die, but some of their offspring will live to run the same gauntlet of decisions when their time to spawn arrives.

Our lives have a common thread with that of Salmolétte because every decision we make determines where we are, where we are going, and where we will end up. We are much like Salmolétte when we are born, but our stream in life is the collective thinking of peer pressure—the need for value, the need to belong. And like Salmolétte, who goes downstream with the current to the ocean, we accept the route of least resistance, the collective thinking of our peers to fulfill our needs. While Salmolétte is in the ocean, most of her compatriots and siblings die and become part of the sea. But Salmolétte and a few others survive and begin swimming against the current, upstream to the place of their beginning—to fulfill their life's purpose of ensuring a new generation.

As we mature, most of us will drown in the ocean of mass thinking, always going with the current, always seeking our sense of value outside ourselves through the acceptance of others who are also drowning in mass thinking. A few, however, will chart their course against the current, against peer pressure, driven by an inner need to find their life's fulfillment in the excellence of achievement. And, like Salmolétte, they leave behind the seeds, the foundations, for even greater achievements by the next generation—for they have dared to risk the unknown, *change*.

I used to think I had easy decisions and difficult decisions. Now I know all decisions are easy, like the snap of fingers. The difficult part is getting ready to make the decision, which is a process of weighing and making many little, often unconscious, decisions— assessments of risk and benefit. We simply cannot get away from decisions. We have no choice because to avoid a decision is still to make a decision, but often not the wisest one. Nevertheless, we are not victims of life; we are products of our decisions. And our willingness to risk change dictates the boldness of our decisions.

In land management, decisions are often difficult to deal with because one is seldom sure who makes them. Decisions just seem to happen; no one seems to be responsible or accountable, and as Bella (1987a) says, our institutions are self-serving in that they distort "unfavorable" data affecting decisions. For example, in thinking about land-management I find that both the California condor and our ancient forests have been relegated to death row. Who made that decision? Why? What does it mean to society to have both the California condor and our ancient forests on death row?

Gentle reader, permit me to digress for a moment from forests to the California condor to make a point:

The condor once graced the sky of southern California, riding the thermals on its 10-foot wingspan. The sky is empty now. The last condor has been captured to give it a stay of extinction but at the cost of its dignity. And what about our dignity? Is our dignity not linked with that of every living thing that shares the planet with us? How can our dignity be intact when we unilaterally erase even one life form from the earth? Extinction is forever, and the species we make extinct have no voice in the decision.

It is difficult for me to write about the condor because I am also writing about myself and society as a whole. The condor, as am I, is far more than simply one of God's creatures. Both the condor and I also represent ecological functions without which the world will be impoverished. True, someone else may be able to take over my individual functional role, but what creature can take over that of the last condor? And we are more than simply creatures that perform ecological functions; we represent the health of the ecosystem—I as an individual in a much smaller way than the last condor.

As the condor becomes extinct, its ecological function becomes extinct, and both the condor and its function become extinct because the habitat characteristics required to keep the condor alive no longer exist. All this means that the whole portion of the ecosystem of which the condor was once a part must now shift to accommodate the condor's annihilation. Do we know what this means in terms of the ecosystem? No. What about the hundreds or thousands of species humanity is making extinct around the world through habitat destruction? How will the ecosystem respond on a global basis to their loss? What repercussions will humanity face as the ecosystem adjusts to their absence? How much of the world must we humans destroy before we learn that we are not, after all, the masters of Nature but exist at Her courtesy?

Viktor Frankl (1963), a psychiatrist who survived Auschwitz and Dachau, understood the feeling of extinction when he wrote (p. 104), "We who lived in concentration camps can remember the men who walked through the huts comforting others, giving away their last piece of bread. They may have been few in number, but they offer sufficient proof that everything can be taken from a man but one thing: the last of the human freedoms—to choose one's attitude in any given set of circumstances, to choose one's own way."

Can the California condor choose its own way behind its prison bars, or is that right also usurped through human arrogance? Frankl (p. 105) also stated that Dostoevski once said, "There is only one thing that I dread: not to be worthy of my sufferings." The condor, by its nature, is worthy of its suffering. The question is, what have we as a society learned from its suffering?

We have relegated the condor to death row for our iniquities and transgressions. Then, to salve our social conscience, we have plucked it from the sky and put it behind bars, and we continue, freely now, to destroy its habitat. Now we will spend money on breeding programs and perhaps purchase a small reservation on which to free a few individuals, should they survive. Would it not be better, however, and more honest, to restore the remaining condors to the dignity of freedom, to watch them, if they are so destined, become extinct in the majesty of the sky, and to accept responsibility for our human failings? How else can we grow in consciousness than to watch the sky slowly become empty of a child of millennia, a creature it took from the beginning of our planet to perfect, to watch the sky become empty by an act of humans—not of God.

If we as a society were called before the throne of judgment today, how would we answer the questions of each species' right to life, of the value of each species in the universal balance, of the stewardship entrusted to us as custodians for those who follow? I don't know how to answer these questions, but I think a good place to start is to restore the condors to their birthright—the freedom and dignity of the sky. Then, perhaps, our consciousness will be raised a little and their suffering and ours will have value. And if the condors survive, it may lead to a time in history when humans and condors can live together. But the question remains: who makes this decision?

## A good decision

Strange as this may sound to your way of thinking, I have always made good decisions. (All my bad decisions have been in hindsight.) I have always made a good decision because I have always made absolutely the best decision I could at that time, under that circumstance, with the data I had on hand. This does not mean, given similar circumstances, I would make the same decision today.

127

It only means that 10 years ago it was a good decision—the best I could do. Today, with 10 years more experience, I can make still a better decision, and 10 years from now an even better one. I am not saying that my decision of 10 years ago was socially acceptable, only that for me it was a good one because it was the best I could do at that time.

You, and I, and everyone else always make the best decisions we can at all times given where we are in life. That does not mean that others will necessarily agree with our decisions or we with theirs. It only calls attention to the fact that I must accept your decision as your best because I cannot judge; I don't know *why* you did what you did. I only know what you did and how that *appeared* to me. And if I were to judge, I could only judge the appearance, which tells me nothing about why you did what you did, and, in my experience, *I am always wrong when I presume to judge.*

An older gentleman in the U.S. Forest Service taught me much about judgment and how I sound to other people. I don't remember his name; it was some years ago. Nevertheless, "thank you." I was giving a speech in Spokane, Washington, about fire in forested landscapes and explaining new data and new points of view. When I was finished, the gentleman came up to me and, with a quivering chin and misty eyes, said, "I've been with the Forest Service 29½ years and I'm going to retire in six months. Do you mean to tell me I've been wrong my whole career?" "No sir, I'm not telling you that at all," I said. "You did the best you could with the data you had on hand. Now, however, with much new data, we can make some different choices, different decisions, than you could during your career." Looking at this good man, listening to his faltering question, it came home to me with searing insight how wrong we are when we presume to judge, and that we are doubly wrong when we presume to judge from hindsight. Everyone does his or her best within his or her level of understanding. It is not what we say so much as how we say it. I now know that I can't "hear" myself when I am speaking, so to be gentle and say what I say with love I have to "feel" how I say things.

This makes me wonder how different the TV program, that I mentioned in the section on judgment, might have been had the moderator gently clarified the issue of ancient forests rather than preying on human dignity to maintain a program rating. Keep in mind that, although he had that choice, he also works for a TV station, and, unbeknownst to him, he may have traded in his choice of heart for the security of his job as dictated by the station and its drive for high viewer ratings. Nevertheless, whether I agree with the program or not, the moderator did the best he could in that circumstance.

## Of captains and cooks

Society is composed of individual human beings much as the compound eye of an insect that is composed of individual facets. Each facet has its own light-sensitive element, each has its own refractive system, and each forms but a portion of the image. As there are as many points of view in the compound eye of an insect as there are facets, so there are as many points of view in a society as there are people, and although everyone is right from her or his point of view, no one person has the complete image. Hugh Prather (1980, p. 93) put it nicely:

> . . . Reality is what reality is, and whatever it may be, it is so vast that no one sees it all. There would be no more intellectual stand-offs if just this much were realized: we are all looking at the same thing and each one of us is seeing something. But since we are standing in different positions, our points of view differ. Fortunately, we can move. And we must if we are to see more.

It is precisely because we each have our point of view, established after we have considered all the data we have and have reached a conclusion, that I can't convince you of anything. If I am to convince you that my point of view is the right one, then I simultaneously have to convince you that your point of view is wrong. But you will resist because your point of view is also correct from your interpretation of "your" data. For example, people seek counselors to get help in changing how they feel, or behave, or both, but they often resist help as we resist new ideas, even new data. As Patterson and Eisenberg (1983, p. 79) explain:

> A client's resistances have helped the client cope with the stresses and pains of life over a long period. At the same time a person's resistances serve him or her well and also result in forms of self-defeat and misery. Asking or demanding that a client give up resistances is the same as asking him or her to give up a reliable, trusted friend who has been with the client since child-

hood. The counselor's efforts to encourage or challenge the client to give up resistances will be resisted.

Although I cannot convince you that you are wrong without stripping you of your dignity, I can give you new data that allows you to reach a new conclusion while maintaining your dignity. What I have done, is raise the value of your making a new decision based on new information. In this way, I can be patient and give you space that allows you to change your mind, for as Prather said, "Fortunately we can move. And we must if we are to see more."

Consider Figure 22. Suppose the ship is sinking. The entire crew,

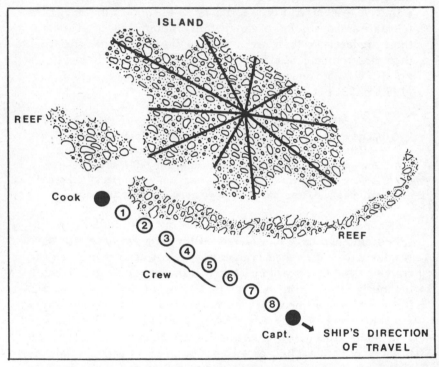

Fig. 22. The ship is sinking, and the entire crew has decided to turn the ship around and head it for the island. Only the cook can see a way to get there. Unless the captain is willing to look at the island from the cook's point of view, the ship will sink and the crew may be lost.

captain and cook included, can see the island, but before they decide to try to get there, they have to decide that is where they want to go. Once that decision is made, the captain looks at the

130

island and sees no way to reach it because the reef prevents them from getting the ship there. The captain then asks the rest of the crew, including the cook, what they see, because each person is peering out of a porthole. The eight crew members all say they see no way to reach the island, but the cook says, "I see a way to get the ship to the island." Each member of the ship's crew is correct from his or her point of view, his or her line of sight. Each sees something they agree is an island, but each sees something different. The only way the captain can see what the cook sees is to move to where the cook is and look from his point of view. That means the captain must have the courage to risk moving from a known, comfortable position to an unknown, uncomfortable position in order to see more.

To save our forests, indeed to save our planet and the human race, we must be willing to risk moving in order to see more, to validate one another's points of view. The world can only be seen in totality when it is seen simultaneously from all points of view, total open-mindedness. To achieve such open-mindedness, we must become students of processes—not advocates of positions. (An excellent example of the evolution of open-mindedness is the career of Aldo Leopold by James Kennedy, 1984).

## *Hidden agendas*

The mind engaged in planning for itself is occupied in setting up control of future happenings. It does not think that it will be provided for, unless it makes its own provisions. Time becomes a future emphasis, to be controlled by learning and experience obtained from past events and previous beliefs. It overlooks the present, for it rests on the idea the past has taught enough to let the mind direct its future course.

The mind that plans is thus refusing to allow for change. What it has learned before becomes the basis for its future goals. Its past experience directs its choice of what will happen. And it does not see that here and now is everything it needs to guarantee a future quite unlike the past, without a continuity of any old ideas and sick beliefs. Anticipation plays no part at all, for present confidence directs the way.

Defenses are the plans you undertake to make against the truth. Their aim is to select what you approve, and disregard what you consider incompatible with your beliefs of your reality. Yet what remains is meaningless indeed. For it is your reality that is the "threat" which your defenses would attack, obscure, and take apart and crucify (*A Course In Miracles, Workbook,* 1975, p. 247).

I will defend my point of view at almost any cost because to me it represents my survival, my integrity. In addition, having "made a stand," I don't want to "look foolish" by "backing down," which really means I don't want to risk rejection by other people. So, I become clever and I view the world as a poker game called "fear." I could probably win the game if I were the only one who played it, but the best I can do is to win a hand now and then because almost everyone plays the same game simultaneously. Unfortunately, the game is dishonest, because we don't play with all our cards on the table; we keep a hidden agenda "up our sleeve." This prevents my developing an open mind because I do not trust anyone else to look out for my welfare—my point of view, which no one else can see— so I justify my own objectives, which makes me narrow-minded and rigid. I have now become defensive, because I must lie about my hidden agenda by appearing to be open and honest. As Emerson once said, "Commit a crime [dishonestly hide an agenda], and the earth is made of glass."

The dynamics of this poker game became clear to me some years ago at a consensus group in which I participated as an observer. At least 30 points of view were represented, because at least 30 people were there. I interpreted three general "collective views," two of which were in opposition over the game's stakes—to cut or not to cut a particular city's watershed. Because I knew nothing about the conflict, even though it had been alive for some years, I had no vested interest in it and could therefore see the collective views. Let's examine my interpretations of them one at a time.

View 1: A most sincere elderly lady, who had lived in this city all her life, had been told in the third grade that the city's watershed, covered with virgin old-growth forest, was her National Heritage and would never be cut. Now she finds people of a land management agency cutting down "her watershed," and she feels that she has been lied to, betrayed. Where the third-grade teacher got the notion of inviolate National Heritage is a moot point. The lady, joined by her son, thinks the land management agency should cease and desist all cutting and road building in the watershed forever. On this she is emphatic.

View 2: The conservation groups that were represented were unanimously opposed to further logging and roading of the water-

132

shed because the virgin, old-growth forest created and protected the pure quality of the city's water supply.

View 3: The people of the land management agency saw the old-growth as an economic commodity that had to be cut and milled or there would be an irreparable loss to the economy because the old-growth forest would rot—an unbearable economic waste.

All three views, each with a stake in the watershed, played the game with a hidden agenda. This was soon apparent as Emerson's comment became clearer and clearer during the two-day session. "Your attitude thunders so loudly I can't hear what you say." The hidden agenda each side was trying to conceal from the others while acting innocently open-minded became clear only because I was not part of the dispute. Although the hidden agendas were never admitted, much less openly laid on the table, they became visible by the strenuousness of defense when someone got too close to the truth. Let's examine them.

View 1: The elderly lady and her son had become rather prominent as distributors of a small newsletter to the group of conservationists interested in saving the watershed's old-growth forest. If the lady and her son won their point of view, they would disappear into the "oblivion from which they came" because, with the issue resolved, the other folks would turn to new issues. This view (my interpretation) became clear because whenever reconciliation seemed possible, the son categorically refused to accept anything that had the appearance of moving the problem toward solution. The hidden agenda seemed to be to keep the issue alive and thereby forestall the feeling of rejection through loss of importance, loss of identity.

View 2: The conservationists were committed to saving the old-growth forest (trees). Each time the people from the land management agency would concede a point that would benefit water quality but not save the trees, the conservationists had to find a new point to argue from, one that sounded valid with respect to clean water and did not mention trees.

View 3: The people from the land management agency were committed to cutting the timber for the reasons I discussed in Part Two of this book. So they submitted to the procedure but with the knowledge of authority on "their side."

Where do we go from here? First, each person and each "collective view" was right from its point of view, from its interpretation of the data. Second, no one in the room really understood consensus.

133

Consensus does not mean something will be enacted, it means that the parties agree to agree on something. And the agreement we ended up with was that something needed to be done, which is where we started. The mission was doomed to failure because *no one* laid *all* his or her cards on the table. This environmental poker game called "fear" is global. The face values on the cards represent the degrees with which we fear change; the stakes in the game are high—the sustainability of our renewable natural resources, such as the forests of the world. Again, Hugh Prather (1980, p. 116) summed it up nicely: "The measure of power is honesty. The measure of success is preparation. The measure of enjoyment is responsibility. The measure of communication is trust." And none of these exist in a poker game called "fear."

Why do we have hidden agendas in the first place? Well, over the years that I worked in the Bureau of Land Management and with the U.S. Forest Service, I noticed that the push was always to meet the self-serving needs of the agency at the expense of human relations. To achieve agency needs, steps were skipped in the process of dealing with one another as people. And this was always justified by the agency's perceived needs of the still larger system—society. The outcome was often a personal confrontation of misunderstandings because we were out of touch with our personal values, which in turn were often in conflict with the agency's goals.

How then do we get rid of our hidden agendas? First, we must recognize and accept responsibility for our personal values because they not only motivate us but also determine our perceptions of each other and of the world. Second, we must accept the validity of our values and then make a conscious choice of whether or not to place them in subservience for the "good of the system" to "keep the system going." Third, we must in clear conscience act on our decision. Only then will we be free of our hidden agendas and the fear they instill, only then will we have a clear view of society and its needs—present and future.

## Emotion and logic

Emotion is defined as: disturbance, excitement, a state of feeling, a psychic and physical reaction (as anger or fear) subjectively experienced as strong feeling and physiologically involving changes that prepare the body for immediate vigorous action. Logic

134

is defined as: a science that deals with the canons and criteria of validity of inference and demonstration, interrelation or sequence of facts and events when seen as inevitable or predictable. Emotion and logic are mutually exclusive. There is no logic in emotion and no emotion in logic; this is a lesson, a critical lesson, that my wife, Zane, taught me.

Emotion is the engine and the energy that drives us, gives us values, feelings. I will discuss only two emotions—love and fear. Love is an expansive, unifying emotion that brings diverse elements of life together under a gentle feeling of an integrated relationship in which all parts cooperate in harmony. Fear, on the other hand, is a contractive, isolating emotion that separates diverse elements of life and shatters relationships into huddled disharmony. Although we think of anger as a separate emotion, it is only violently projected fear. A point to consider is that when we are fearful or angry we are always "out of control." Think, for example, of extreme anger—rage—and "temporary insanity" in a court of law. A person in a rage is indeed out of control and insane.

When Zane used to get angry at me, I would say "Babe, there's a logical explanation," and she would promptly "blow up." Why? It took me a long time to understand that *her emotions were valid,* and that *logic was not required to validate them.* My "logical approach" was an invalidation of her emotions. I was in fact saying, "your emotions are invalid because you don't understand how to look at the world." Well, I did not understand that both views are valid because they are different and not substitutable. Negative emotion must be validated and allowed to run its course before logic can be accepted. Recall, for example, the last section "Hidden Agendas" (p. 116). We ended with the consensus that something needed to be done, which is where we had started. We made no apparent headway because the entire two-day meeting was mired with "hidden agendas"; no one exposed "real emotions," his or her fear of loss. Negative emotion can only be brought to logic when all parties are open and honest—where love, trust, and respect prevail.

Negative emotions must be validated before they can be brought to logic. Logic is the steering wheel that allows us to negotiate the values contained in our emotions. Let's look again at the section "Hidden Agendas." We started out with about 30 points of view, 30 individual emotional views, and ended up with three collective emotional views. But the three collective emotional views were really false, "decoy" emotional views, so the real emotional views

135

could not be validated by anyone because everyone denied their existence. Had the real emotional views been expressed, we might have been able to understand each other and validate each other's set of values. Then, and only then, could our racing engines (emotion) be slowed to cruising speed so that we could use the steering wheel and road map (logic and negotiation) to arrive at a satisfactory conclusion built on love, trust, and respect.

Emotion is the feeling, and logic is the looking of the world. Each is only half. Together they give us sight by allowing us to *see* the world. We shall remain in darkness, however, until we you and I have enough love, trust, and respect for each other that we may bring our emotions and logic to wholeness—light.

As management of our forests becomes more and more of a public concern with public meetings, written responses to management plans, and legal contests in court, it is imperative to understand and account for the difference between emotion and logic. I have found, with the help of my wife, Zane, that one of the most insidious acts of violence that we perpetrate against each other as human beings is in not listening to one another. What goes unheard is how we feel—our emotions. For an example, let's go back a moment to the TV program that I was on, the one that was to air the issue of our ancient forests. There was an old lady on the program who tried in vain to be heard, but the moderator ignored her. Even after we were off the air and she tried to tell him how she was feeling, he ignored her. In the end, just to be heard, perhaps only by herself, she spoke out loud to no one, she spoke into space. She may as well have been alone in the universe.

As I said in the Introduction, all we have in the world as human beings is each other, and all we have to give each other is each other. We are each our own gift to one another and to the world; we have nothing else of value to give. I cannot give my gift, however, if there is no one to receive it, if there is no one to hear. Therefore, if we listen—*really listen*—to one another and validate each other's feelings (emotions) even if we don't agree, we can begin to manage our forests without the violence and pain of not being heard.

### A gift from Elisabeth

In 1969, Elisabeth Kübler-Ross published a book *On Death and Dying,* which simultaneously is a book "On Life and Living."

Elisabeth described five stages a terminally ill person goes through when told of her or his impending death: denial and isolation, anger, bargaining, depression, and acceptance. We will examine these stages here, and then I'll relate them to our thought processes and to change:

1. Denial, refusing to admit reality, trying to invalidate logic, is the first stage a terminally ill person goes through. Denial leads to a feeling of isolation, of being helpless and alone in the universe. At some level, however, the person knows the truth but is not yet emotionally ready or able to accept it.

2. Anger, which is a violent projection of fear, can be called emotional panic. The person is emotionally out of control because she or he can no longer control circumstances.

3. Bargaining is when a person attempts to bargain with God to change the circumstances, to find a way out of having to deal with what is.

4. Depression is a somewhat different type of issue because there are two types of depression. In the first type, a person is in the process of losing everything and everyone she or he loves. The second type of depression is one in which a person is no longer concerned with past losses, such as a job, but is taking impending losses into account, such as leaving loved ones behind. I suppose this may be similar to a state of resignation in which a person is simply submissive to the inevitable. Resignation is sterile, without hope.

5. Acceptance, the final stage, is creative and positive. With acceptance, returns a trust, a faith, in the goodness, the rightness of the outcome. Acceptance allows us to acknowledge our problem, which allows us to define our problem, which allows us to solve our problem. But first *we must accept what is,* which is to: *know the truth that sets us free* (John 8:32).

Now let's see how understanding these stages of dying not only helps the living to understand the dying but also helps the living to understand the living—Elisabeth's gift to us. Although we are alive, we die daily to our ideas and belief systems, and in so doing, we go through the five stages of dying that Elisabeth described. They are necessary as they prepare the way for change, a dying of the old thoughts and a birth of the new:

1. Denial of or resistance to change is the first stage of a dying belief system. An example appeared in a story by Ken Slocum (*The Wall Street Journal,* 11 March 1986):

How big a role should the recreation industry play in the Rocky Mountain West when promoting tourism means turning away from timber and mining, industries that helped build the economies of the mountain states? It's a hotly debated question in Idaho, where a lot of people see recreation as an antidote for an economy lagging behind the national recovery.

Walter C. Minnick, president of Trus Joist Corp. of Boise, argues that lumbering should actually be curtailed in areas where logging roads and timber cutting threaten tourism. "The Rocky Mountain West is the marginal timber-producing area of North America because of low rainfall, long winters, and rugged mountains that make roads expensive to build," he says. "It's foolish to subsidize and try to prevent the decline of one industry at the cost of compromising the future of an unsubsidized industry (tourism) that's growing."

Disagreeing sharply is Robert T. Hitchcock, President of Evergreen Forest Products Inc., New Meadows, Idaho. He says environmentalists have encouraged stories of a wounded timber industry for their own political ends. "One of the ploys we see environmentalists using is to say recreation is the true backbone of the economy, and in order to increase and improve that, we have to cut less timber." Adds Mr. Hitchcock: "Our industry is not dead and dying."

We isolate ourselves when we do not accept change. We become defensive, fearful, and increasingly rigid in our thinking; we harden and close our minds. If I become defensive about anything, if I start to form a rebuttal before someone is finished speaking, if I filter what is said to hear only what I want to hear, I am in this denial stage.

2. Anger is the violent projection of uncontrollable fear. I am so afraid of change, of the dying of my old belief system, that I become temporarily insane: "I can't cope with this!" My anger, however, is not aimed at you; it is aimed at my inability to control the circumstances that I find so threatening.

3. Bargaining is looking for a way to alter the circumstances based on "acceptable" conditions. In forestry, I call it fertilization, which is an impatience with Nature's timetable so we look for an "acceptable" shortcut. We bargain with Nature, "If I do this, will you do that?"

4. Depression is when we become resigned to our inability to control or change the "system," whatever that is, to suit our desires. We feel helpless and deliberately give up trying to alter circum-

stances. We become "victims" of outside forces and our defense is to become cynical—distrustful of human nature and motives. A cynic is a critic who stresses faults and raises objections but assumes no responsibility. A cynic sees the situation as hopeless and is therefore a prophet of doom who espouses self-fulfilling prophecies of failure regardless of the effort invested in success.

5. Acceptance of what is, for example an unplanned change, allows us to define the problem and to solve it. Acceptance of the problem, however, must come before a solution is possible.

Why do we fear change so much? We resist change because we are committed to protecting our existing belief system. Even if it is no longer valid, it represents past knowledge that is safe. We try to take our safe past and project it into an unknown future by skipping the present that represents change and holds accountability. Thus, when confronted with change, we try to control the thoughts of others by accepting "approved" thoughts and rejecting "unapproved" thoughts. We see such control as a defense against change because change after all is "in the mind." As George Bernard Shaw said, "My own education operated by a succession of eye-openers each involving the repudiation of some previously held belief." Change is the death of an accepted, "tried and true" belief system through which we have coped with life; it is our comfort zone that has become synonymous with our identity. Have you ever noticed, for example, that when someone is asked the misstated question "What are you?" they almost inevitably tell what their profession is—their safe identity. When we get "too comfortable" with our belief systems, we might think of the turtle who only gets ahead by sticking its neck out. For only a person who takes risks is free.

## Our human experience

I have tried to define the kaleidoscope of fear we call life by examining some of the causes of fear. I have also pointed out that we can alleviate our fears if we change our thinking. For example, we must recognize and accept that we cannot judge except falsely; so we must let go of judgment, which ultimately is isolation from evidence. Second, we must learn to be present, in the here and now; fear is a past experience whose possible recurrence is projected into the future. It is impossible to be afraid in the present. As Mahatma

139

Gandhi said, "If we will take care of today, God will take care of tomorrow." Third, we must remember the two emotions, love and fear, and that we cannot be afraid of that which we learn to love. There are no "enemies" "out there," only other frightened people. To this end, Gandhi stated, "Intolerance betrays lack of faith in one's cause."

Gandhi spoke of tolerance; so once again, let's put people from land-managment agencies into perspective with a quote from Bella (1987a, pp. 369–370):

> Organizations tend to systematically distort information in self-serving ways. Such distortions do not depend . . . [on] deliberate falsifications by individuals. Instead, people who are competent, hard-working, and honest can sustain systematic distortions by merely carrying out their organizational roles. Unchecked by outside influences or the undeniable realities of catastrophic failures, organizational systems can sustain self-serving distortions. The potential for catastrophic consequences is significant.
>
> A technological culture faces two choices. First, it can wait until catastrophic failures expose systemic deficiencies, distortions, and self-deceptions. . . . Second, a culture can provide social checks and balances to correct for systemic distortions prior to catastrophic failures. This second more desirable alternative, however, requires the active involvement of independent engineers and scientists [and other dedicated professionals and lay people]. They must ask "unfavorable" questions and pursue "unfavorable" inquiries. Without such initiatives, checks and balances are undermined and catastrophic possibilities are likely to increase as the scope and power of organizational technology expands.

I am going to close this section with excerpts from a speech dealing with change that Norman Cousins (1975, p. 103, 104, 112) gave to professional foresters. Titled "The Fatalists [non-risk takers] *versus* The Doers [risk takers]," it was later published in the *Journal of Forestry,* from which I quote:

> . . . It's impossible to conceive of any problem beyond the reach of human intelligence that is definable, because to define a problem gives you access to the answer. We went to the moon not because of our technology; we went to the moon because of our intelligence, because of our imagination. Someone had to imagine

that it was worth doing. When we imagined that it could be done and that it ought to be done, then everything else became the servant. The technology became the servant of the imagination. . . .

It is unscientific and unhistorical, therefore, to say that we are locked in. We are not locked in so long as (a) we can define the problem, (b) we are willing to attack it. . . . The thing that separates fatalists from other people is that the fatalist is unwilling to struggle; he's unwilling to make the attempt. So the real issue of our time, it seems to me, is that the human race today is divided between those who are willing to make the fight and those who are not. It has nothing to do with knowledge. Both sides, I think, are equally well informed; both sides have access to a wide body of knowledge. But, ultimately, it's a philosophical problem: are we going to make the attempt? The answer, of course, depends on what our view of the human species is, what our understanding of the human spirit is. . . . the question before all of us is, 'can we have an inspired response to our problem, beginning with the environment?'. . . .

Again, it can be done if enough people wish it to be done. The crisis . . . is in the will and the imagination.

## Part Four

# WE ARE AS FREE AS OUR IMAGINATION

*Two kinds of landscapes are worth looking at—*
*those that man has never touched,*
*and those in which man has gained harmony.*
—Paul B. Sears

I titled Part Two "As we think, so we manage," and at another level this saying also applies to Part Four. We can either be held hostage by old, rigid belief patterns or we can risk new, innovative ideas about managing forests. Although we want to think like employers in forest management, we must think like employees of the future because there always is an individual and collective price for what we do, both within and between generations. And we must remember that *we have one ecosystem that simultaneously produces and sustains a multitude of products, including ourselves.* In this sense, we talk about our responsibility to future generations, but we need to act on the ability of future generations to respond to the legacy of options we leave them. It is therefore imperative that we understand and account for both the short-term and long-term ramifications of our decisions; this can only be done by thinking of them simultaneously, as an old bedouin taught me.

I was working in Egypt in 1963–1964, and I wanted to go to a particular "black hill" I had been told about. The hill was in the desert about 200 miles southwest of Alexandria. The desert in this part of Egypt is flat and sandy with areas of desert pavement as far as the eye can see (Photo 41). We had traveled by jeep a ways when my bedouin guide told me to steer about three inches to the right. I looked at him as though he had sunstroke. Three inches! What difference could three inches possibly make? He didn't even have a map! I was finally persuaded to make this "insignificant correction." Well, two days later we were at the "black hill" (Photo 42),

Photo 41. Desert pavement, small pebbles that protect the sand from blowing away, in the Western Desert of Egypt. (Photograph by author.)

and there my guide told me to get out my map. I spread the map on the hood of the jeep and learned about humility. My guide drew a triangle and showed me that a correction of three inches near Alexandria had saved us about 50 miles worth of fuel and water on our way to the black hill (Fig. 23). The further we predict into the trackless future, the more conscious and clear we must be of our motives, our goals, and our data.

## *Sustainable forests = sustainable harvest*

We must have a sustainable forest before we can have a sustainable yield (harvest). Said in reverse, we cannot have a sustainable yield until we have a sustainable forest. We must have a sustainable forest to have a sustainable yield, and we must have a sustainable yield to have a sustainable industry, and we must have a sustainable industry to have a sustainable economy, and we must have a sustainable economy to have a sustainable society. Put another way, we must first practice sound "bio-economics" (the economics of maintaining a healthy forest), before we can practice sound

146

Photo 42. "Black hill" in the Western Desert of Egypt. (Photograph by author.)

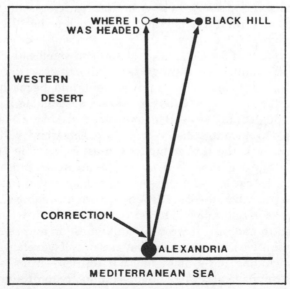

Fig. 23. A Bedouin guide in Egypt taught me the essential lesson of traveling through the trackless sands of time in the present and future simultaneously. He made a three-inch correction near Alexandria that saved us about 50 miles of fuel and water when we reached the black hill 200 miles out into the Western Desert. (Not to scale).

147

"industrio-economics" (the economics of maintaining a healthy forest industry), before we can practice sound "socio-economics" (the economics of maintaining a healthy society). And it all begins with a solid foundation—a sustainable forest—just like the parable given by the Buddha about the wealthy but foolish man who only wanted the third story of his house (see p. 37).

We are not now headed toward sustainable forestry because we are training plantation managers, not foresters. A forester manages a forest. We are liquidating our forests and replacing them with short-rotation plantations. We will have foresters only when we have sustainable forests in which we manage not just trees, but processes. Everything Nature has done in Her design of forests adds to diversity, complexity, and stability through time. We decrease diversity, complexity, and stability through time by redesigning forests into plantations.

We have a unique forest in the Pacific Northwest, yet we are teaching and practicing European plantation management. We need to develop our own forestry in updated, revitalized university curricula that stress forest ecology, not product harvest, that teach good writing, speaking, and people skills, in addition to timber cruising and sale layout. We need to learn to see the forest as the factory that produces raw materials—such as healthy soils to grow trees and filter water; pure water to drink, with which to irrigate crops, and for electricity; salmon and steelhead, deer and elk; and the countless other products and amenities we derive from forests. We need to learn about reinvestments into the machinery of the forest factory so our mills will have a sustainable harvest of timber through time. We need to understand that Nature cannot be constrained to absolutes, that sustained yield is a trend within some limits, that even the timber industry must be flexible and continually change over time. And our schools of forestry must become leaders on the cutting edge of research, management, and human relations rather than the last bastions against inevitable change.

We can have a sustainable forest, but only if that is what we are committed to and only if we constantly question and re-evaluate what we think we know along the way and only if we retain all of the pieces—including old-growth (ancient forests)—from which to learn. We can have a sustainable forest industry to produce wood products for people, but only if we redesign industry to operate, in fact, within the sustainable limits set by the forest, not by people. In both cases, we must learn humility, which means we must learn to

148

be teachable. In both cases, we must become students of processes—not advocates of positions. In both cases, our schools of forestry and the Congress of the United States must be leaders, rather than anchored resisters of change. In both cases, we must work together for a common goal, with a common commitment: a sustainable forest for a sustainable industry for a sustainable environment for a sustainable human population.

## Why old-growth

There are many valid reasons to save old-growth forests from extinction, as many, perhaps, as there are for saving tropical forests. One is that our forests of the Pacific Northwest are beautiful and unique in the world (Waring and Franklin 1979). Another is that the old-growth trees of the Pacific Northwest inspire spiritual renewal in many people and are among the rapidly dwindling living monarchs of the world's forests (Photo 43). They are unique, irreplaceable, and finite in number, and they shall exist precisely once in the world today because whatever we create in the redesigned forest will be different. We can perhaps grow large trees

Photo 43. Old-growth island surrounded by forest plantations of various ages. (USDA Forest Service photograph by J.F. Franklin.)

over two or three centuries, but no one has ever done that on purpose. Such trees will not be Nature's trees; they will be humanity's trees. And although they may be just as beautiful as those created by Nature, they will be different in the human mind (Anonymous 1986a, Baker 1986, Jones 1986, Kelly and Braasch 1986). A third reason is that a number of organisms, such as the spotted owl and the flying squirrel, either find their optimum habitat in these old-growth forests or require old-growth structures, such as large snags and fallen trees, to survive (Forsman et al. 1984, Franklin et al. 1981, Harris 1984, Harris et al. 1982, Maser and Trappe 1984, Meslow et al. 1981). And a fourth reason is that old-growth forests are the only living laboratories through which we and the future may be able to learn how to create sustainable forests—something no one in the world has so far accomplished. Let's examine this in more detail.

As a living laboratory, old-growth forests serve four vital functions. First, old-growth forests are our link to the past, to the historical forest. The historical view tells us what the present is built on, and the present in turn tells us what the future is projected on. As stated by Jan Christian Smuts (1926, p. 213), "The whole [the forest], if one may say so, takes long views, both into the future and into the past; and mere considerations of present utility do not weigh very heavily with it." *To lose the old-growth forests is to cast ourselves adrift in a sea of almost total uncertainty with respect to the sustainability of future forests.* We must remember that knowledge is only in past tense; learning is only in present tense; and prediction is only in future tense. To have sustainable forests, we need to be able to know, to learn, and to predict. Without old-growth, we eliminate learning, limit our knowledge, and greatly diminish our ability to predict.

Second, we did not design the forest, so we do not have a blueprint, parts catalog, or maintenance manual with which to understand and repair it (Maser and Trappe 1984b). Nor do we have a service department in which the necessary repairs can be made. Therefore, how can we afford to liquidate the old-growth that acts as a blueprint, parts catalog, maintenance manual, and service station—our only hope of understanding the sustainability of the redesigned, plantation forest?

Third, we are, as I said earlier, playing "genetic roulette" with forests of the future. What if our genetic simplifications run amuck, as they so often have around the world? Old-growth forests are thus imperative because they—and only they—contain the entire genetic code for living, healthy, adaptable forests.

150

Fourth, intact segments of the old-growth forest from which we can learn will allow us to make the necessary adjustments in both our thinking and our subsequent course of management to help assure the sustainability of the redesigned forest. If we choose not to deal with the heart of the old-growth issue—sustainable forests, we will find that reality is more subtle than our understanding of it and that our "good intentions" will likely give bad results.

Although there are many valid reasons to save old-growth forests, there is only one reason that I know of for liquidating them—short-term economics (Overton and Hunt 1974). Economics, however, is the common language of western civilization; is it not therefore wise to carefully consider whether saving substantial amounts of well-distributed old-growth forests is a necessary part of the equation for maintaining a solvent forest industry?

*Can we really afford to liquidate our remaining old-growth forests?* I have often heard that "We can't afford to save old-growth, it's too valuable and too many jobs are at stake." I submit, however, that *we are only limited by what we think we can't do.* We must be exceedingly cautious that economic judgment does not isolate us from the evidence that without sustainable forests, we won't have a sustainable forest industry. Therefore, if we liquidate the old-growth forests— our living laboratories—and our plantations fail, as plantations are failing over much of the world, industry will be the bath water thrown out with the baby (Overton and Hunt 1974).

## *If we really want the spotted owl to survive*

The northern spotted owl has become a surrogate for old-growth forests, a symbol in the struggle of conflicting values—short-term economics versus all other human values of old-growth forests. On the emotional side, the following titles help define the struggle: Cut the trees and damn the recreation (Poole and Williamson 1983); Who-o-o-o cares about old forests, owls pit naturalists vs. loggers (DeYonge 1985); Forest giants falling fast (Evans 1986); Logging peril to spotted owl said listed in federal report (Kadera 1986a); Spotted owl set-asides may wipe out 1,300 jobs (Kadera 1986b); Both camps unhappy with spotted owl decision (Anonymous 1986b); Lumber barons use owls for scapegoats (*Corvallis Gazette-Time's View* 1986); Spotted owl chosen symbol for endangered old growth (Wilkinson 1986); Oregon's billion-dollar bird (Sullivan 1986); Owls or old-growth? (Taylor 1987).

At issue here are conflicting values and the emotional interpretations they give rise to. As stated in *A Course in Miracles* (Manual for Teachers 1975, pp. 42–43):

> Perhaps it will be helpful to remember that no one can be angry at a fact. It is always an interpretation that gives rise to negative emotions, regardless of their seeming justification by what appears as facts. Regardless, too, of the intensity of the anger that is aroused. It may be merely slight irritation, perhaps too mild to be even clearly recognized. Or it may also take the form of intense rage, accompanied by thoughts of violence, fantasized or apparently acted out. It does not matter. All of these reactions are the same. They obscure the truth, and this can never be a matter of degree. Either truth is apparent, or it is not. It cannot be partially recognized. Who is unaware of truth must look upon illusions.

The foregoing brings me to the crux of the issue. The spotted owl is the symbol for the survival of the old-growth forest, but what does it really symbolize? The spotted owl is called an "indicator species" because its presence supposedly indicates a healthy old-growth forest, but what does it really indicate? *The spotted owl may be seen as a symbol for the survival of old-growth forests, but in reality it is an indicator species for the planned extinction of old-growth forests.* Although the spotted owl was selected as the symbol of old-growth with good intentions, the results are bad if the objective is to save the owl because the real issue is not the owl. The real issue is the economics of extinction (Chasan 1977; Overton and Hunt 1974; Robbins 1984, 1985, 1988; Worster 1979)—the planned liquidation of old-growth forests for short-term economic gains.

If we really want spotted owls to survive, then we must want old-growth forests to survive also because on the scientific side there is evidence beyond a reasonable doubt that northern spotted owls require the unique structural components of old-growth forests (Forsman et al. 1984, Franklin et al. 1981, Irwin 1986). Where is scientific data to the contrary? This is not evident, however, from the management plans for public lands. Old-growth set-asides, as now planned, will create self-destruct islands of time-limited old-growth in a sea of young-growth plantations. Unless a portion of the existing mature forests also is set aside to replace the old-growth as it falls apart with age or by unplanned catastrophe, the spotted owl is doomed. And then the only difference is time if a portion of the young-growth forest is not also committed to replace the mature

152

forest as needed to maintain quality spotted owl habitat. *We are planning spotted owl habitat in terms of absolute minimums and the old-growth cut in terms of flexible maximums.*

Easwaran (1986, p. 134), discussing the historian Arnold Toynbee, put the issue of the economics of extinction into perspective, "Toynbee asks in detail, why did twenty-six great civilizations fall? And his conclusion: Because they could not change their direction, their way of thinking, to meet the changing challenges of life." Can society afford the environmental costs of the economics of extinction? Have we become so myopic in our economic view that we are willing to risk losing the ability to have sustainable forests for the short-sighted, short-term, economic windfall to be had by cutting the remaining old-growth trees?

### And God gave us only so much water . . .

Water is a physical necessity of life. The world's supply of quality water is therefore precious beyond compare. The amount and quality of water available for human use is largely the result of our strategies for management of watersheds. But water quality and quantity is not a primary concern in timber harvest (Photo 44). We

Photo 44. Clearcut and hot burn showing that water quality is not a primary concern when timber is harvested. Note the completely exposed second-order stream in the bottom. (Photograph by author.)

153

the people of the United States do not even seem to realize that our water comes from forested watersheds. Even the prehistoric ground water we are pumping came from forested watersheds. Our water, and therefore most of our electricity, is a forest product just as surely as is woodfiber. A curious thing happens, however, when water flows outside the forest boundary: we forget where it came from. We spend our time fighting over who has the "right" to the last drop (Chasan 1977, Crosson 1979) while paying only lip service to the supply—the health of the forested watersheds. For example, McCartney (1986) wrote:

> A concrete canal ribbons its way 190 miles over red rock mountains and scorched sand, defying the laws of both gravity and economics, representing both the past and future of watering the West.
> 
> The umbilical cord called the Central Arizona Project carries water uphill at 4 mph from the Colorado River to bursting, thirsting cities. It is the last and most expensive of all the great federal waterworks, a $3.6 billion aqueduct conceived as a way to irrigate the desert and hailed as the final answer for Arizona's needs. . . .
> 
> "Most of the West is going to have to pay more," said water director Frank Brooks, the pioneer of Tucson's tactics.
> 
> "Historically, what we've done with all our natural products is use the cheap stuff first. It works the same way in a coal mine, the same way with oil. [Note that both examples refer to mining.] I think there's certainly much greater awareness now that *all of our natural resources are exhaustible—even water*" [emphasis mine].

In addition to insensitive management of the world's watersheds, we are mining the world's water supply. As stated by Chasan (1977, p. 69), "One might suppose that people would automatically conserve the only naturally occurring water in a virtual desert, but one would be wrong. Land and farm machinery have capital value. Water in the ground, like salmon in the sea, does not. Just as salmon are worth money only if you catch them, water is worth money only if you pump it." And we are damming, diverting, and channeling the world's rivers to "tame" and to "harness" them for human use that, again, is based on economics rather than nurturance of the life-giving water (Highsmith and Kimerling 1979, Petts 1984). As with old-growth forests and soil, we are mining the resource, practicing the economics of extinction with the world's supply of fresh water (Worster 1985). As stated in the Office of Technology Assessment report "Water-related Technologies for Sustainable Agriculture in

154

U.S. Arid/Semiarid Lands" (Kendrick et al. 1983, p. 10), under "Watershed Management":

> Two major classes of watersheds occur in the Western United States: 1) highland watersheds, located in the major mountain ranges and consisting of the untimbered "alpine" zone (above the timberline) and the timbered "montane" zone; and 2) lowland watersheds consisting of grass- or brush-covered valleys and plains. Watershed-management technologies are designed to increase surface runoff by vegetation removal or replacement or by other surface modifications.[5]

Note that nothing is said about managing vegetation to prevent erosion, to increase the infiltration of water to recharge the underground aquifers and become purified in the process. In fact, the report further states (pp. 9 and 10) under the headings "Technologies Affecting Precipitation and Runoff" and "Weather Modification":

> ... *hydrologic research activities and priorities should reflect the fact that most of the annual surface runoff and ground water recharge in the West comes from the mountain snowpack* [emphasis mine] (Photo 45).

---

5. See Appendix 2 for long quote.

Photo 45. Winter snowpack in the high mountains is the source of most of our water from forested watersheds. (Photograph by author.)

Weather-modification technologies are designed to increase the amount of precipitation over that which occurs naturally. This is done by injecting artificial nucleating agents, such as silver iodide, into suitable air masses. The two weather-modification technologies that have received the most attention are those involving: 1) winter storms that cross the major mountain ranges of the Western United States, producing the snowpack of the mountain watersheds; and 2) the summer cumulus clouds that produce both rain and hail, often in large amounts over limited areas. Of the two, precipitation augmentation from winter storm systems by "cloud seeding" appears to show the most promise. This technology has been developed within a solid scientific framework creating a body of knowledge that should facilitate future advances.

What, may I ask, would "cloud seeding" do to other parts of the environment? What would be the unanticipated, long-term, cumulative effects of such environmental tampering for a short-term economic gain? And under "Water Supply and Use" (pp. 6 and 7) the report makes several points:

1. "Available estimates of water supply and use indicate that almost half of the Western United States is experiencing water-supply problems in relation to demand."

2. "Present trends and experience indicate that every additional drop of water conserved, and thus available, enables more growth and development, raising demand levels further. Effective water-use management will necessitate attention to demand as well as supply aspects of water use."

3. "Because these components interrelate, a change produced by technology in one component of the cycle will inevitably affect other components."

4. "Short-term climatic fluctuations affecting water supply can be accommodated in management and planning processes through statistical analysis of past trends; there is no reliable method for predicting long-term fluctuations."

5. "In the short history of this country, there have always been more lands and more resources to develop and a philosophy that technology could supplement natural resources when needed."

6. "Stretching resources to accommodate the West's continuing growth while protecting existing patterns of water demand may require levels of technical input no longer economically feasible."[6]

---

6. See Appendix 2 for long quote.

Is water to become the ultimate economic/environmental club with which we bludgeon each other? The only solution is an environmental one—sound ecological landscape/watershed management that first and foremost nurtures soil and water health, lest everything else becomes unhealthy (Brash 1979, Dunne and Leopold 1978, Thomas et al. 1956). Like migratory birds and anadromous fish, environmental crises know no national boundaries. Soil, water, and air form a seamless whole—the thin envelope we call the biosphere, which is all we have in all the universe . . . our past, our present, and our future.

In addition to sick watersheds, we also face pollution problems (Maddock et al. 1984). For example:

> Poland suffers from the worst environmental pollution in the world and 12 million of its people live on the "verge of ecological catastrophe." . . .
>
> "The threat to the environment in Poland is believed to be the greatest in the world," said the 350-page study, drafted by ecology experts of the Academy of Social Sciences. . . .
>
> The water in more than 90 percent of the nation's rivers is too polluted to drink, and 70 percent of the water in the country's biggest river, the Vistula, is even too polluted for industry, the study said (Anonymous 1985).

And *The Oregonian* carried a story by Tagliabue (1986), "Parts of poisoned Rhine flow lifelessly." "Scientists said . . . that roughly 185 miles of the Rhine River, from Basel, Switzerland, to Mainz, West Germany, had suffered serious ecological damage as a result of the accidental release of poisonous chemicals." The *Corvallis Gazette-Times* elaborated on the story (Anonymous 1986c), "The Rhine was so 'massively upset' by a toxic chemical spill that it may need a decade [to] recover, and new breeding stocks of fish will not be introduced for years. . . ." These are past and present problems; what about the future?

> An agricultural expert with the National Academy of Sciences predicts pollution of water by agricultural chemicals will become the predominant natural resource problem to agriculture in coming years.
>
> For a half century, soil conservation has been the dominant natural resource issue of agriculture. Charles Benbrook, Executive Director of the Academy's Board on Agriculture, predicted it will rapidly be supplanted by water quality protection. The two

157

values can come into conflict, he said, when controlling erosion exacerbates water problems.

Several states are monitoring quality of groundwater polluted by seepage of chemicals through soil into groundwater. This summer [1986] the Environmental Protection Agency will begin the first national survey of groundwater, yielding a better data base with which to measure the problem. . . . (Anonymous 1986d).

As with any problem, there are solutions, but we tend to look for solutions only where the symptoms become obvious. For example, I used to live in an old mobile home. You know the kind: it leaked immediately every time a dark cloud appeared on the horizon. Finding where the leak ended—on my desk or over my pillow in bed—was no problem, but finding the source of the leak was often so difficult that I had to repair the entire "waterproof" coating on the roof—and then hope.

The problem with our watersheds begins with the headwaters, the first-order stream and its watershed (Fig. 24). A first-order

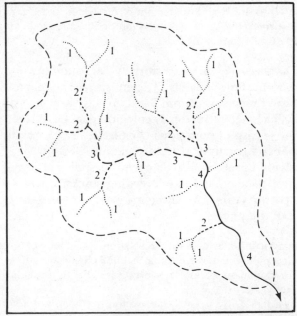

Fig. 24. Stream order in a typical watershed. The majority of stream mileage is in first- and second-order tributaries in all watersheds of western Oregon and western Washington (from *Water in Environmental Planning*, by Thomas Dunne and Luna B. Leopold. Copyright © 1978 W. H. Freeman & Co. Used with permission.)

watershed is always a special case; in fact it is probably the only part of the land we manipulate that has ecological integrity because it is the headwaters, and therefore controls the initial water quality for the whole watershed. A first-order watershed, by definition, is unique unto itself. A second-order watershed is unique among second-order watersheds, but it is a common denominator, an integrator, of the first-order watersheds that created it. A third-order watershed is unique among third-order watersheds, but it is a common denominator of the first- and second-order watersheds that created it, and so on.

Our thinking, our view of the world is generally limited to a kaleidoscope of special cases because we choose to focus on "discrete" parcels of real estate. If we deal only with special cases, a mile of stream, for example, we perpetuate our inability to understand both that particular mile of stream, the entire stream, and the watershed as a whole. If, on the other hand, we deal with a particular mile of stream—special case—in relation to the whole watershed—common denominator—we enhance our ability to understand both the mile of stream and the watershed because each is defined by its relation to the other. Our understanding of how a section of stream relates to the whole watershed is like understanding how a single chair relates to a room. If we stand in the doorway and survey the room, we will see the chair in the room, but when we focus only on the chair we can no longer see the room. Unfortunately we do not see that the first-order watersheds are the initial control of water quality for our domestic water supplies. We therefore cut timber right down into the stream bottoms of both first- and second-order streams because the timber is thought to have greater immediate economic value than the water (Photo 46). And besides, fish, such as salmon and steelhead, don't live that high so these small streams are of no visible economic importance.

In addition to our lack of vision with respect to nurturance of our watersheds, we are also bleeding water from the land with roads the same way cuts in the bark bleed sap from sugar maple (Fig. 25). The U.S. Forest Service, for example, wants to expand its road network in the 119 million acres of publicly owned forests. As stated by Basden (1987) in *The Oregonian*, "*Initially set up to manage timberlands and protect watersheds, the Forest Service is best understood as the world's largest socialized road building company* [emphasis mine]. More than 340,000 miles of roads have been constructed under its auspices, more than eight times the mileage of the entire U.S. Interstate

Photo 46. First-order watersheds are the quality control of our drinking water, but the water does not hold the same value to the timber industry as does woodfiber. (USDA Forest Service photograph.)

Fig. 25. Unless water infiltrates deeply into the soil, it runs down hill and reaches a road cut that brings it to the surface, collects it into a ditch, and puts it through a culvert to begin infiltrating again. The water then meets another road cut, and so on. Water is sometimes brought to the surface three, four, or more times. Water is purified by its journey through the deeper soil not by surface flow. Roads therefore have an impact on the hydrology of a watershed and on the purity of the water that reaches human habitations.

Highway System." And Blumm (1987), also in *The Oregonian,* stated, "The Forest Service's 1985 renewable resource program promises construction of some 77,000 miles of new road[s] ... in the 39 national forests in Oregon, Washington, Idaho and Montanta." Blumm goes on to say that, "Some 24,000 miles of the proposed 77,000 miles of the new Northwest forest roads will be constructed in Oregon." The world at the equator is 25,000 miles in circumference; thus 340,000 miles is 13.6 times around the world at the equator. If we add the other 77,000 miles, an additional 3.1 times around the world, that is the equivelant of 16.7 times around the world on forest service roads. And this does not count "temporary roads." How many acres of land are "permanently" out of timber production to accommodate this road system? If we figure, as Blumm (1987) suggested, that 4.5 acres of productive land are lost per mile of road, that means the already existing 340,000 miles of road equals 15,300,000 nonproductive acres. Adding another 77,000 miles of road (3,465,000 acres), would bring the total acres out of production to 18,765,000. If the 77,000 miles of new road are added to the 340,000 miles already built, that would take more than one-seventh of the Forest Service's 119 million acres out of production. And this does not even include those acres out of production because of private logging roads or logging roads on other public lands, such as those on the Bureau of Land Management. How much more—if any—can society afford?

If you are wondering why I've spent so much time on water and what all this has to do with a sustainable forest, the answer is simple. Forest roads are constructed primarily to harvest timber, and these roads affect the quality, quantity, distribution, and effects of water in the soil of the watershed. Enough roads over time can alter the soil-water cycle of entire forested landscapes and as soil-water cycles are altered so is the forest's ability to grow. Remember, the quality and quantity of water is one of the four cornerstones of forestry that we consider to be a constant. Even if water were a constant, which it isn't, we introduce a variable with construction of the first logging road. And we compound the variable from then on by constructing and maintaining logging and access roads to harvest timber. In addition, logging and plantation management alter the water regime; the altered water regime affects how the forest grows. We can thus create a cycle of watershed degradation over time that alters the soil-water regime and in turn alters the sustainability of the forest that in turn affects the soil-water regime, etc.

161

We can continue to degrade our watersheds and impoverish our water supply, or we can risk abandoning our conventional thought pattern and—with a strong, concerted commitment—reverse the trend. The choice is ours and so are the consequences. In the final analysis, we must remember that God gave us only so much water.

## The enemy in the courtroom

Although each court case, however small, in our struggle to redefine our land ethics is a stitch in the changing tapestry of the redesigned world, it is of diminished value if we lose our integrity, our self-respect (=dignity) in the "legal process." I have been an "expert" witness in federal court several times during my 13 years with the Bureau of Land Management, and to date, all I have seen the court used for is an arena in which to legalize character assassination, ignorance, and a point of view—a power struggle that is fueled by short-term economics and resistance to change.

What happens to a society whose land ethics must be decided in court? What happens to a society that obeys the letter of the law and violates the heart of the law? First, we perceive each other as enemies. Us (public) against them (U.S. government) or vice versa on public lands, or me against you, or you against me on private lands. We might ask who owns the land over which we have the arrogance to fight—public or private; are we not only custodians for those who follow? Second, we go to court with any and every legal standing we can find, almost always procedure, seldom substance. And from what I've seen, the "ends justify the means" even when we crucify each other on the witness stand to "win" a victory at the cost of human dignity (Maser 1984). But what have we won? Because human values can neither be legislated nor legalized, do the ends really justify the means when my "victory" is legally forcing you to "change" your mind, termed "compliance," so I won't have to change mine? Remember that I can only *force* you to "change" your mind by coercion, by legally controlling you, and I can only control you or anyone else through the art of humiliation.

The question is, "who's right" when we are all right from our own points of view? If everyone is right, then who's wrong? Because no one is wrong, we cannot argue any case on "right" or "wrong" (Allen and Gould 1986). Right or wrong is always a human judg-

162

ment, and judgments, by definition, can only deal with appearances, not with reality. Everyone loses when land issues are "settled" by judgments of right or wrong because, again, judgments can deal only with appearances and everyone appears to have the right point of view. In addition, we go to court over procedural matters, so the land loses in the end, which means all of humanity has lost. If, on the other hand, the court could assess and would rule on the long-term ecological health of the land, then the land and humanity could win.

The arguments I have seen always dealt with short-term economics—how much can I get in products from the land for as little capital outlay as possible? The same statement is valid for both industrialists and conservationists. Conservationists, for example, could bid for the land the same as the industrialists, buy it and simply not cut the timber. There is no need for a court to intervene as umpire if both sides play by the same rules and neither side cheats. The problem is both sides cheat and justify it by "I'm right; my enemy is wrong." This is no different than a world at war; each nation, each army, each person is sure God is on its side. Did you ever stop to think that we might all be wrong?

Let's look at a typical case dealing with a patch of old-growth forest. The U.S. attorneys and the industrialists' attorneys argue either that it is "just one sale of old-growth" of which there is plenty, but they don't know how much or where, or they argue about lost jobs, which is also an untenable argument when mills are being automated to eliminate jobs and save money. For example, the *Corvallis Gazette-Times* carried a story "Mill modernization will cost 60 jobs": "Willamette Industries plans to modernize its Albany paper mill, and says the project will cost 60 workers their jobs when it is finished in 1987" (Anonymous 1986e). In either instance, the argument is one of special cases and is out of relation to the whole, the common denominator—the relation of the stand to be cut to other immediate old-growth stands and the watershed and landscape on the one hand and nurturance of mill workers on the other.

With respect to timber, both the U.S. government attorneys and those for industry use generalizations about theoretical lack of harm to the land by liquidating old-growth forests—with no data— and demand specific data to "prove" old-growth is needed for ecosystem health. Conservationists must "prove" the impacts of cumulative effects based on scientific data while industrialists can legalize disregard based on procedure. A final government-industrialist argument is that "the land is already damaged so a little more won't hurt."

There has to be a better way to manage land. The burden placed on a court judge—without a thorough scientific background—to make ecological decisions that will have a cumulative affect on the world forever is incomprehensible. Whenever a person works for the U.S. government, whether as a federal judge, a politician, or a scientist, she or he must pass the tests described in the eulogy Senator William Pitt Fessenden of Maine, delivered on the death of Senator Foot of Vermont in 1866:

> When, Mr. President, a man becomes a member of this body he cannot even dream of the ordeal to which he cannot fail to be exposed;
>> of how much courage he must possess to resist the temptations which daily beset him;
>> of that sensitive shrinking from undeserved censure which he must learn to control;
>> of the ever-recurring contest between a natural desire for public approbation and a sense of public duty;
>> of the load of injustice he must be content to bear, even from those who should be his friends; the imputations of his motives; the sneers and sarcasms of ignorance and malice; all the manifold injuries which partisan or private malignity, disappointed of its objects, may shower upon his unprotected head.
>
> All this, Mr. President, if he would retain his integrity, he must learn to bear unmoved, and walk steadily onward in the path of duty, sustained only by the reflection that time may do him justice, or if not, that after all his individual hopes and aspirations, and even his name among men, should be of little account to him when weighed in the balance against the welfare of a people of whose destiny he is a constituted guardian and defender (Kennedy 1961, p. 247).

Two years after Senator Fessenden delivered this eulogy, his vote to acquit Andrew Johnson brought about the fulfillment of his own prophecy.[7]

Who is the enemy in the courtroom? Is it the U.S. attorney? the industrialist? the conservationist? the judge? the witness? who?

---

6. Senator Fessenden's vote to acquit President Andrew Johnson under the Articles of Impeachment sealed his political fate and he was never again elected to the United States Senate.

There is no human enemy. The enemy in the courtroom is fear and ignorance, an enemy it takes the utmost courage to face, for each of us must face our own fear and ignorance in the depths of his or her soul. John F. Kennedy (1961, p. 245–246) stated it eloquently:

> . . . demonstrations of past courage nor the need for future courage are confined to the Senate alone. Not only do the problems of courage and conscience concern every officeholder in our land, however humble or mighty, and to whomever he may be responsible—voters, a legislature, a political machine or a party organization. They concern as well every voter in our land—and they concern those who do not vote, those who take no interest in Government, those who have only disdain for the politician and his profession. They concern everyone who has ever complained about corruption in high places, and everyone who has ever insisted that his representative abide by his wishes. For, in a democracy, every citizen, regardless of his interest in politics, "holds office"; every one of us is in a position of responsibility; and, in the final analysis, the kind of government we get depends upon how we fulfill those responsibilities. We, the people, are the boss, and we will get the kind of political leadership, be it good or bad, that we demand and deserve.
>
> These problems do not even concern politics alone—for the same basic choice of courage or compliance continually faces us all, whether we fear the anger of constituents, friends, a board of directors or our union, whenever we stand against the flow of opinion on strongly contested issues. For without belittling the courage with which men have died, we should not forget those acts of courage with which men . . . have lived. The courage of life is often a less dramatic spectacle than the courage of a final moment; but it is no less a magnificent mixture of triumph and tragedy. A man does what he must—in spite of personal consequences, in spite of obstacles and dangers and pressures—and that is the basis of all human morality.
>
> To be courageous . . . requires no exceptional qualifications, no magic formula, no special combination of time, place and circumstance. It is an opportunity that sooner or later is presented to us all. Politics merely furnishes one arena which imposes special tests of courage. In whatever arena of life one may meet the challenge of courage, whatever may be the sacrifices he faces if he follows his conscience—the loss of his friends, his fortune, his contentment, even the esteem of his fellow men—each man must decide for himself the course he will follow. The stories of past courage can define that ingredient—they can teach, they can offer hope, they can provide inspiration. But they cannot supply courage itself. For this each man must look into his own soul.

# Alice in objectiveland

Few people either know what an objective is or know how to set one. In explaining objectives, I have liberally drawn on two articles that I have written (Maser 1985, 1987).

An objective is defined as something towards which effort is directed. There is a saying in Nova Scotia, "If you don't know where you're going, any path will take you there." Thus, without clearly defined objectives, we take "potluck" with the outcome, just as Alice did in Wonderland (Carroll 1933). When Alice met the Cheshire-Cat in Lewis Carroll's story of Alice's Adventures in Wonderland, she asked the Cheshire-Cat:

> "Would you tell me, please, which way I ought to go from here?"
> "That depends a good deal on where you want to get to," said the Cat.
> "I don't much care where—" said Alice.
> "Then it doesn't matter which way you go," said the Cat.
> "—so long as I get somewhere," Alice added as an explanation.
> "Oh, you're sure to do that," said the Cat, "if you only walk long enough" (p. 75–76).

A carefully defined objective tells us where we are going, what the value is of getting there, and what is the probability of success. It is a measure of our achievement. Too often, however, we set objectives by "sleeve shopping." Sleeve shopping is going into a store to buy a jacket and deciding which jacket you like by the price tag on the sleeve. To set an objective, first determine what you want by the perceived value of the outcome. Second, make the commitment to pay the price. Third, determine the price of achieving the outcome. Fourth, figure out how to fulfill your commitment and make the commitment to do so. Alexander the Great gave us an excellent example of how to set an objective. When he and his troops landed by ship on a foreign shore and found themselves badly out-numbered, he sent some men to burn the ships, so the story goes. Alexander then ordered his troops to watch the ships burn, after which he told them, "Now we win or die."

An objective has six components, and to frame the objective, each must be accounted for. They include: (1) what do you want? (2) where do you want it? (3) why do you want it? (4) when do you

166

want it? (5) how much (or many) do you want? and (6) how long do you want it (or them)? If a component is missing, the objective will be achieved by default rather than by design. Only when all these questions have been asked and concisely answered, do we have a clearly defined, clearly stated objective. Only now are we ready for planning.

Once our objective is framed, we know where we want to go; we have some idea of the value of going there; and we can calculate the probability of arrival. Next we have to determine the cost, make the commitment to pay it, and then commit ourselves to keeping our commitment. Now we are ready to do battle.

As we strive to achieve the objective, we must accept and remember that the objective is fixed, as though in concrete, but the plan to achieve the objective must remain flexible and changeable. A common human tendency, however, is instead to change the objective—devalue it—if it cannot be reached in the chosen way. It is much easier, it seems, to devalue an objective than it is to change an elaborate plan that has shown it will not achieve the objective as originally perceived.

Although it is we who define our objectives, it is the land that limits our options. So we must keep these limitations firmly in mind. At the same time, we must recognize that the reverse side of these seemingly arbitrary limits is the dependability of the conditions they represent. They can be viewed either as nuisance snags in our preferred path, or as solid ground on which to build new paths. As previously stated, *nature deals only in short- and long-term trends— not in absolutes.* Second, habitat (food, cover, and water) is a common denominator among species; and we can use this knowledge to our benefit. Third, sustainable forests require sound, long-term ecological objectives before short-term economic objectives can be considered.

One of the main reasons industrialists have succeeded in liquidating the majority of the old-growth forests in the Pacific Northwest is because they are the only ones with well-defined objectives. They know exactly what they want—old-growth timber; where they want it—at the mill; why they want it—to make money on a free, finite resource; when they want it—now; how much they want—all of it; how long they want it—as long as it will last, to the last tree.

Let's look at a short case study that appeared in Oregon State University's *The Daily Barometer* (Anonymous 1986a). The article,

167

titled "The Millennium Grove Massacre" dealt with a 1,300-acre parcel of land that once contained Douglas fir trees that were estimated to have been between 800 and 900 years old, making them the oldest known stand of trees in the state:

> In 1984, the U.S. Forest Service sold about 200 acres in the heart of the stand to Willamette Industries. Nearly 150 acres of the sale have been clearcut. The remaining 56 acres were scheduled for cutting this summer. When the Oregon Natural Resources Council (ONRC) brought suit earlier this year to halt all cutting in the area, however, Willamette Industries apparently decided to force the issue.
>
> Last week, the company selectively cut the largest and oldest trees in the stand, effectively nullifying the ONRC suit. The trees are to be turned into plywood and fiber board. Apparently the company has broken no laws, and plans to complete the clearcut ahead of schedule will undoubtedly go forward.

Officials of Willamette Industries, right or wrong, were the only ones who had clearly defined objectives, and they carried them out boldly, within their legal bounds. These episodes, all too common with finite natural resources, smack of the courtroom where, in cases of natural resources, procedure and the letter of the law—rather than substance and the heart of the law—seem to prevail.

The sad part of this case is that when I examined the logged site, I found that only about 50 percent of each old-growth tree had been used because they were so rotten. The other 50 percent was on firewood piles or burn piles. Furthermore, the stand was not old-growth in the ecological sense; it was scattered old-growth trees surrounded by mid-aged trees. The latter could have been logged while leaving the old-growth trees standing.

To these confrontations that gain little but enmity, I have a solution: sustainable forests through restoration forestry (to be discussed later). Without restoration forestry, the words in honor of Paul Bunyan carved on the wall of Mahlon Sweet airport in Eugene, Oregon, will cease to be a beacon for the future and will pass into the cemetery of history: "From days before yesterday to days after tomorrow—from the winter of blue snow to the summer of green apples—from the roaring valley of the Wiscons to the bearded valley slopes of the Willamette—thus have Paul's mighty strides set our pace."

## *". . . It was then that I carried you."*

Occasionally someone gives us a beautiful gift, but we don't immediately see how it relates to our life. My father gave me many such gifts when I was young, yet a few of them am I only now able to fully appreciate. The following quote as I have used it here fits this dilemma. So, gentle reader, if you can be patient, by the end of this section you will see how it relates.

> One night a man had a dream. He dreamed he was walking along the beach with the LORD. Across the sky flashed scenes from his life. For each scene, he noticed two sets of footprints in the sand; one belonged to him, and the other to the LORD.
>
> When the last scene of his life flashed before him, he looked back at the footprints in the sand. He noticed that many times along the path of his life there was only one set of footprints. He also noticed that it happened at the very lowest and saddest times in his life.
>
> This really bothered him and he questioned the LORD about it. "LORD, you said that once I decided to follow you, you'd walk with me all the way. But I have noticed that during the most troublesome times in my life, there is only one set of footprints. I don't understand why when I needed you most you would leave me."
>
> The LORD replied, "My precious, precious child, I love you and I would never leave you. During your times of trial and suffering, when you see only one set of footprints, it was then that I carried you" (The gift of an anonymous author).

Dr. Seuss (1971) gave us the gift of humility through his Truffula Trees:

> But those *trees!* Those *trees!*
> *Those Truffula trees!*
> All my life I'd been searching
> for trees such as these.
> The touch of their tufts
> was much softer than silk.
> And they had a sweet smell
> of fresh butterfly milk.
>
>      . . .

169

In no time at all, I had built a small shop.
Then I chopped down a Truffula Tree with one chop.
And with great skillful skill and with great speedy speed,
I took the soft tuft. And I knitted a Thneed!

. . .

And at that very moment, we heard a loud whack!
From outside in the fields came a sickening smack
of an axe on a tree. Then we heard the tree fall.
*The very last Truffula Tree of them all!*

. . .

"So . . .
Catch!" calls the Once-ler.
He lets something fall."
It's a Truffula Seed.
It's the last one of all!
You're in charge of the last of the Truffula Seeds.
And Truffula Trees are what everyone needs.
Plant a new Truffula. Treat it with care.
Give it clean water. And feed it fresh air.
Grow a forest. Protect it from axes that hack.
Then the Lorax
and all of his friends
may come back."

What have we learned? "Ravage in the rain forests, loss of 100 acres a minute threatens earth's climate. Clearcutting wastes one million acres a year and dooms one species of wildlife to extinction per day in the Amazon region. The land will become desert in a few years after trees in the lush Peruvian forest have been felled" (Anonymous 1986f). "Slash burning blamed for hike in sea carcinogens" (Jones 1986). "Floods, cancer seen if ozone loss unchecked" (Anonymous 1986g). "Acid rain not the, or not the only, villain" (Haines 1986). "Nuclear winter adds to futility of war" (Williams 1986). "Chernobyl fallout may destroy Lapps' way of life. 'According to some experts, nearly half of the Lapland reindeer will be contaminated [with radioactive cesium] for at least five years,' says Brian Jackman . . . who studied the [Chernobyl] disaster . . . 'If these estimates are correct, the future of the Lapps as a separate people is bleak indeed" (Anonymous 1987a). "Scientists say we've lost war with insects. The human race, packing more pesticides than common sense, has lost the war with the insect kingdom and inadvertently created armies of superbugs 'nothing can kill,' top

170

insect experts warn. 'The short-sighted and irresponsible use of pesticides . . . is producing strains of monster bugs. There are now about 30 species that nothing can kill'. . . ." (Anonymous 1987b). "Teaching Poseidon [the Greek God of the sea] to turn a profit. . . . today, mortals have penetrated the walls of his undersea fortress. Poseidon has been deposed" (Schiefelbein 1979). According to Schiefelbein, there is a vast storehouse of food, minerals, and energy beneath the waves just waiting to be exploited. "Scientists warn tropical forests face destruction. More than a dozen Soviet scientists linked arms with U.S. environmental groups . . . in asking their governments to join forces against the destruction of tropical rain forests. . . . scientists warned that almost all the world's tropical forests will be destroyed in the next 30 years unless trends are reversed, and 'it is difficult to avoid the conclusion that up to one billion people will starve to death in the tropics.' . . . scientists are seeking U.S.-Soviet cooperation . . . to halt the destruction, which they believe eventually will alter global climate, create deserts and lead to the extinction of millions of species of plants and animals" (Anonymous 1987c).

These excerpts are a mirror image of one part of us; unfortunately it is the most visible image. And as can be seen in the excerpt, "Teaching Poseidon to turn a profit," we cling to our arrogance and take ourselves with us wherever we go. In our times of world trial and suffering, in our times of darkness, would we not be wise to seek humility and ask the Lord to carry us one more time?

With humility, the other part of us can also be mirrored, as exemplified by the story of a French shepherd, Elzéard Bouffier, the man who planted hope and grew happiness (Giono 1967):

> The countryside had not changed. However, beyond the deserted village I glimpsed in the distance a sort of greyish mist that covered the mountaintops like a carpet. Since the day before, I had begun to think again of the shepherd tree-planter. "Ten thousand oaks," I reflected, "really take up quite a bit of space." I had seen too many men die during those five years [of the First World War] not to imagine easily that Elzéard Bouffier was dead, especially since, at twenty, one regards men of fifty as old men with nothing left to do but die. He was not dead. As a matter of fact he was extremely spry. He had changed jobs. Now he had only four sheep but, instead, a hundred beehives. He had got rid of the sheep because they threatened his young trees. For, he told me

171

(and I saw for myself), the war had disturbed him not at all. He had imperturbably continued to plant. . . .

He had pursued his plan, and beech trees as high as my shoulder, spreading out as far as the eye could reach, confirmed it. He showed me handsome clumps of birch planted five years before—that is, in 1915, when I had been fighting at Verdun. He had set them out in all the valleys where he had guessed—and rightly—that there was moisture almost at the surface of the ground. They were as delicate as young girls, and very well established.

Creation seemed to come about in a sort of chain reaction. He did not worry about it; he was determinedly pursuing his task in all its simplicity; but as we went back towards the village I saw water flowing in brooks that had been dry since the memory of man. This was the most impressive result of chain reaction that I had seen. These dry streams had once, long ago, run with water. Some of the dreary villages I mentioned before had been built on the sites of ancient Roman settlements, traces of which still remained; and archaeologists, exploring there, had found fishhooks where, in the twentieth century, cisterns were needed to assure a small supply of water. . . .

In the direction from which we had come the slopes were covered with trees twenty to twenty-five feet tall. I remembered how the land had looked in 1913: a desert . . . Peaceful, regular toil, the vigorous mountain air, frugality and, above all, serenity in the spirit had endowed this old man with awe-inspiring health. He was one of God's athletes. I wondered how many more acres he was going to cover with trees. . . .

I saw Elzéard Bouffier for the last time in June of 1945. He was then eighty-seven. . . .

On site of the ruins I had seen in 1913 now stand neat farms, cleanly plastered, testifying to a happy and comfortable life. The old streams, fed by the rains and snows that the forest conserves, are flowing again . . . more than 10,000 people owe their happiness to Elzéard Bouffier.

When I reflect that one man, armed only with his own physical and moral resources, was able to cause this land of Canaan to spring from the wasteland, I am convinced that, in spite of everything, humanity is admirable. But when I compute the unfailing greatness of spirit and the tenacity of benevolence that it must have taken to achieve this result, I am taken with an immense respect for that old and unlearned peasant who was able to complete a work worthy of God.

Elzéard Bouffier had learned two important lessons: how to live in the present so he was undisturbed by either WW I or WW II and how to give a gift so he never worried about which tree germinated and grew. A gift is free; it has no conditions. If, for example, I give you a book and you give it to someone else, for whatever reason, then I have given a gift twice. If the second person gives the book to a third person, then I have given a gift three times. If, on the other hand, I give you a book on the condition that you read it and keep it, I have given you a condition—a prison cell—not a gift. I have traded a book to you for your compliance with my expectations of your behavior. I have used the book to control you.

Because we insist on trading with our natural resources, we think of them as a commodity of which I must get "my share" before you do. This mental, emotional prison to which we have exiled ourselves precludes our seeing the world as other than an unpredictable, frightening, competitive, combat zone in which no one and nothing can be trusted.

Elzéard Bouffier asked only to be allowed to plant trees in a land no one wanted, and he gave a gift of love through the trees he planted. Is it not possible that we too can see beyond short-term exploitive, plantation mangement? Is it not possible for us—who call ourselves "foresters"—to plant forests and grow hope and happiness? Can we not change our thinking so once again there may be two sets of footprints in the sand?

## Restoration forestry

Liquidating old-growth forests is not forestry; it is simply spending our inheritance. Nor is planting a monoculture forestry; it is simply plantation management, and plantation management is all we are currently practicing. We are trying very hard to make a gigantic monotypic plantation out of most of the Northwest's forests. *The only time we will practice "forestry" is when we begin to see the forest and we begin to restore its health and integrity—restoration forestry.*

Restoration forestry is the only true forestry. We use the forest—remove products and nutrients—and then we restore its vitality, its sustainability so that we can remove more products in time without impairing the forest's ability to function. From the time we cut the original old-growth, we must continually practice restoration

173

forestry. Anything else is not forestry. Anything else is simply abuse of the system for short-term economic exploitation (Robbins 1984, 1985, 1988). Today, for example, we practice European plantation management, but we don't want to accept the results of such practices. In other words, we want to be a special case with Mother Nature; we want to "have our forest and exploit it, too."

Let's see what concepts restoration forestry might include before we discuss how we might accomplish it in practice. Restoration is defined as the act of restoring or returning to its original condition; renewing. Thus, we have to know what the original condition was; this is another value of defining the various unmanaged successional stages within our forests, such as young-growth forest, mature forest, and old-growth forest—how they differ, how they are similar. To do this, we have to maintain some original, unmanaged old-growth forest, mature forest, and young-growth forest as parts catalog, maintenance manual, and service department from which to learn how to practice restoration forestry.

These unmanaged forests also are living laboratories that simultaneously serve as living dictionaries and living libraries where we can define such things as productivity of soil for specific types of forest sites. For example, the Soil Science Society of America (1984, p. 8), defines soil productivity as "The status of a soil with respect to its ability to supply nutrients essential to plant growth." And the USDA Forest Service manual (1986, 2521.05) defines soil productivity as, "The inherent capacity of a soil for supporting growth of specified plants, plant communities, or sequence of plant communities." Limitations are necessary since no soil can produce all plant communities or crops with equal success nor can a single system of management produce the same effect on all soils. The way we use the term productivity emphasizes the capacity of soil to produce crops and is expressed in terms of yields. What does this really mean in terms of sustainable forests with respect to soil type, gradients of moisture, elevation, and latitude, slope, and aspect within the forests of the Pacific Northwest? How will we ever know without a well-distributed system of living laboratories?

Restoration forestry is, by definition, the exact opposite of the plantation management we practice today. In plantation management, costs are hidden and deferred to the next rotation or human generation (Perry, in press; Perry and Maghembe, in press); in restoration forestry, on the other hand, there are no hidden, deferred costs. Restoration forestry is pay-as-you-go forestry that

174

more closely follows Nature's blueprint in maintaining a self-repairing, self-sustaining forest. Product extraction is maximized in traditional plantation management and sustainability of the forest is minimized; in restoration forestry, however, sustainability of the forest is maximized and product extraction is "optimized" at a level and in a way that does not impinge on the sustainability of the forest. Today we are applying 100 percent of what we know about product extraction and utilization in plantation management and only about 10 to 20 percent of what we know about sustaining the forest. *Restoration forestry demands that we use 100 percent of what we know about sustaining the forest and 100 percent of what we know about product harvest and use, but the former must be maximized while the latter must be optimized* (Fig. 26).

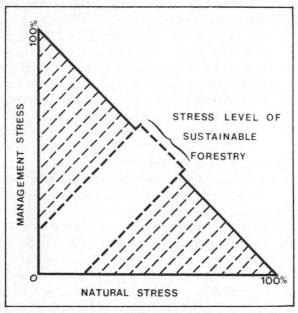

Fig. 26. We can manage the forest for products on a sustainable basis with restoration forestry provided we do not exceed the stress threshold beyond which the forest may not be repairable. The higher the natural stress the lower the management stress must be; the lower the natural stress the higher the management stress can be—but always within the limits of a sustainable forest.

All of this means that we must reassess the value in which we hold the land. For example, money is as previously mentioned, symbolic of the value we place on something. The amount of money we spend on a car, house, or vacation is a measure of the value we place on those items. Isn't it strange that we spend more money on cars, houses, and vacations than we do in our care of the land? We spend many, many times more money to extract products from the land (including extractive and utilization research and technology) than we spend in protecting and sustaining the system that is responsible for the products in the first place. That we maximize our expenditures in extracting the products and minimize our expenditures in caring for the land can be seen clearly in the economic models and managment plans on forested lands.

Let's examine some possibilities more closely. Suppose we compare renting a home from someone with buying a stand of old-growth or young-growth timber, which in essence is renting public lands for a profit. When we rent a home, we come to an agreement on the price and then we pay a deposit of some percent to cover any damage we may cause. If we cause damage, we forfeit an appropriate amount of the deposit; if not, our deposit is returned when we leave. Why don't we do something similar on public lands? A timber company buys the timber (rents public lands for the profit in the timber) and must pay a deposit, say 10 percent of the value in the timber, to be held in escrow until all their logging and other contractual obligations have been fulfilled and they are released by the contracting officer. If the company has lived up to the contract, their deposit is returned; if not, damages are assessed and restitution is made to the public by using whatever portion of the deposit is necessary to repair the damage. The same thing could be done with contract tree planting, or any contractual work on public lands. The point is: *whoever makes a profit off public lands needs to be totally accountable for any and all damages they cause at no cost to the tax-paying public.*

In addition, the public needs to begin sharing part of the financial burden of public land stewardship. This could be done by paying an annual fee for the use of public lands for such things as mushroom hunting, bird watching, fishing, hiking, skiing, etc. Fee hunting on public lands is already on its way (Monroe 1986, Thomas 1984).

Our understanding of forest sustainability is also skewed by our focus on the theoretical money-product base of plantation management. We simply do not understand or accept that, all too often, parts of forests—such as trees—are not interchangeable, not substitutable. Forests are not automobiles in which we can tailor artificially substituted parts for original parts. Trees may look similar but they don't necessarily function in a similar manner. Plochmann (1968, p. 25) addressed this problem in Germany:

> One further drawback, which is typical of all pure plantations, is that the ecology of the natural plant associations became unbalanced. Outside of the natural habitat, and when planted in pure stands, the physical condition of the single tree weakens and resistance against enemies decreases. This problem is compounded because we [in Germany] do not have control of all the ecological factors when we place trees in a strange environment; it may prove to be more favorable to tree enemies than to trees. For example, we imported the Douglas fir from your country [United States], and with the trees brought in two fungi. In North America, these fungi do little damage to Douglas fir, but in our country the destruction was severe. The result was repeated insect and fungi catastrophes which destroyed large forests.
>
> Our experiences with even three or four generations of pure conifer stands, mainly outside of their natural distribution area, shows that their cultivation is possible, their management in many ways easier, and their economic results even better than those of the natural mixed forests. But they show, too, that the risk involved is high, and that the productive capacity of the soil can be lowered markedly. The dangers involved can be checked only partially by artificial means. Artificial fertilization, chemical insecticides and fungicides, and the use of the most appropriate seed origin may lower the risk but cannot eliminate it. Besides, these costs will consume large parts of the anticipated profit. These experiences led us to the conviction that even from the economic point of view, plantations of pure conifer forests have to be restricted to the areas where they occur naturally; that means the subalpine spruce region, and to the best and most stable sites where the danger of a decreasing production capacity of the soil and of other disturbances are low or do not exist.

*And yet we continue to ignore data from around the world, for whatever reason,* as exemplified by an article in the *Corvallis Gazette-Times:*

> The remote nation of Nepal has a serious deforestation problem. In Oregon there lives a citizen who raises fast-growing hybrid poplar trees. Sen. Mark O. Hatfield, R-Ore., chairs the Appropriations Committee. The committee earmarked $2.28 million in its fiscal 1986 foreign operations bill to send 2.5 million Oregon poplar tree cuttings to Nepal.

177

Nothing new there, you say? Happens all the time? Ah, but in this case, Nepal resisted: These poplars might not grow well there. The Agency for International Development also resisted, listening to one of its foresters who argued that the project would be "completely unrealistic, a waste of money" and "an act of extreme folly" because of transport, land availability and refrigeration problems.

Hatfield was determined. "He really believes that this is an important and valid development project," said aide Rick Rolf. . . .

. . . A feasibility study that AID ordered in January—but which committee aides said was a stalling tactic—reported that Nepal does indeed need "a tree such as a poplar" that can be used as fuel, animal feed, brushwood and a soil holder and windbreak. The study, headed by Argonne National Laboratories, said that other varieties of trees also should be explored (Anonymous 1986h).

Nothing was said in the article about using native trees, and remember, some individuals of the U.S. AID mission were largely responsible for Nepal's deforestation problem in the first place. As I said before, I watched the progress of deforestation while I was working in Nepal during 1966–1967.

It is important that we once again discuss the unity of all things before we go on to examine some ideas of how a forest functions that in turn may allow us to understand how to restore a forest. We will turn again to Capra (1975, pp. 209, 286, 291):

Thus modern physics shows us once again—and this time at the macroscopic level—that material objects are not distinct entities, but are inseparably linked to their environment; that their properties can only be understood in terms of their interaction with the rest of the world. . . .

The bootstrap philosophy constitutes the final rejection of the mechanistic world view in modern physics. Newton's universe was constructed from a set of basic entities with certain fundamental properties, which had been created by God and thus were not amenable to further analysis. In one way or another, this notion was implicit in all theories of natural science until the bootstrap hypothesis stated explicitly that the world cannot be understood as an assemblage of entities which cannot be analysed further. In the new world view, the universe is seen as a dynamic web of interrelated events. None of the properties of any part of this web is fundamental; they all follow from the properties of the other parts, and the overall consistency of their mutual interrelations determines the structure of the entire web. . . .

The Eastern sages, therefore, are generally not interested in explaining things, but rather in obtaining a direct non-intellectual experience of the unity of all things. This was the attitude of the Buddha who answered all questions about life's meaning, the origin of the world, or the nature of *nirvana,* with a "noble silence" The nonsensical answers of Zen masters, when asked to explain something, seem to have the same purpose; to make the student realize that everything is a consequence of all the rest; that "explaining" nature just means to show its unity; that, ultimately, there is nothing to explain.

The crux of maintaining diversity within a forest is that things must exist before they can be in relation to one another, part of the unity of all things (Franklin, in press). I am, in this case, specifically including the diversity of processes in the concept of diversity within a forest because diversity—both structural and functional—either maintains or alters the speed and direction of succession and hence the resulting plant community. For example, a forest does not have a single state of equilibrium nor is it characterized by a single deterministic pattern of recovery (Botkin 1979). Botkin wrote:

> Throughout the history of ecology, including the most recent decades, ecologists have tended to believe that the stability of natural ecosystems was metaphorically like the stability of a simple mechanical system. This metaphor has been used in a mathematically formal way in a great many discussions of ecosystem theory and management. . . . This metaphor is incorrect and can lead to undesirable management policies. Clearly, if this view of stability is wrong in practice, it must be wrong for ecosystem theory. An ecosystem, like a jack pine forest, is more likely to persist on the landscape with certain rates of disturbance than with others, and it will disappear altogether without perturbation. The persistence of biota on the landscape is a central concern of discussions of stability in ecology and is clearly central to many ecological investigations.
>
> . . . We must abandon the concept of static stability in both theory and management of natural ecosystems. There may be a variety of alternative concepts, but I have suggested that we replace the concept of static or mechanical stability with two others: (1) the persistence of an ecosystem with bounds [within limits] and (2) the recurrence of specific ecosystem states. With these concepts we can focus on our real concern: the probability that ecosystems will persist on the earth's surface. By recognizing the real nature of our concerns, we recognize that change and stability are linked together . . . (p. 10).

179

Restoration forestry can be built on the above two premises: (1) that within some limits, some trend, a forest will persist, and (2) given the chance, a specific ecosystem state, plant community, or successional stage will recur. This means that if we accept the first premise we will allow the second to fulfill itself, but not on all acres all of the time and perhaps not even on our timetable all of the time. Bear in mind that we can guide Nature gently, as we might a child, but if we try to force Her, like a child, She will surely resist and do things we do not want and over which we have no control. Nature is Her own master; She is not our servant; She may, given a chance, be our partner.

Restoration forestry, as I see it, is the only hope the world has for sustainable forests and healthy watersheds. Before Nature will cooperate as our partner, however, we must meet Her conditions:

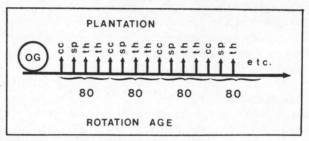

Fig. 27. Linear plantation management in which the old-growth (OG) is clearcut (cc). The clearcut site is then prepared and planted (sp); the young-growth forest is precommercially thinned once (first th); commercially thinned once (second th); and finally clearcut (cc) again at the end of 80 years. The plantation cycle then starts over and over and over and over, with the focus always on maximizing woodfiber production.

(1) We must shift our focus from products to the forest (Figs. 27 and 28); (2) We must balance the energy we remove from the forest in products by allowing the forest time to repair its processes and reinvest nutrients—some of the "product capital"—into itself in a way that is available to the next forest (Sachs and Sollins 1986) (Fig. 29A). And we must simultaneously minimize and account for cumulative effects or we will alter plant communities in ways we do not want (Fig. 29B); (3) We must accept and learn to manage in long-term trends, which means industry must be flexible and accountable to the forest that produces its raw materials; (4) Given a chance, the most desirable successional stage will probably recur, and the probability is higher in some areas than in others. It is there-

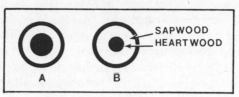

Fig. 28. Schematic representation of the heartwood:sapwood ratio in a cross-section of a slowly grown, old-growth Douglas-fir tree (A) and an equal-diameter fast-grown, plantation Douglas-fir tree (B). This shift in heartwood:sapwood ratio between the old-growth tree and the young-growth, plantation tree alters the dynamics of decomposition, nutrient cycling, habitat values, and many other processes that make plantations less stable ecologically over time. The sapwood, rich in carbohydrates, is rapidly consumed and decomposed by organisms; the heartwood, composed mostly of lignin, is long-lasting and important in the formation of soil humus and mycorrhizae.

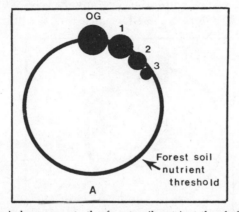

Fig. 29-A. The circle represents the forest soil nutrient threshold (maintenance budget) required to maintain the site in a forest community through time. When the old-growth forest (OG) is cut, the first plantation (1) does very well because it draws on the surplus budget of stored, available nutrients (refer to figs. 13 and 16) and relatively intact belowground, ecological processes. The second plantation (2) does less well because there is less nutrient capital from which to draw, and the ecological processes have suffered greater disruption. The third plantation (3) does poorly because the nutrient budget is becoming depleted and the belowground, ecological processes have become severely disrupted by intensive management. If, at this point, the forest is replanted and left to grow *without further human intervention* until it reaches the old-growth stage, the soil nutrient capital and the belowground ecological processes can repair themselves and the forest again becomes self-sustaining. The forest can then be harvested and a new plantation cycle initiated. The maintenance budget of forest soil nutrients must retain its integrity to make this management scenario possible.

181

fore wise to carefully select areas for different intensities of management and harvest based on the sustainability of the forest at the selected level of harvest; (5) We must develop practices appropriate for the management of our own forest and cease trying to force incompatible practices on our forest; (6) We must practice landscape management with the aid of satellites; and (7) In humility we must accept Nature as our teacher.

Assuming we meet these conditions, how does restoration forestry work? Restoration forestry combines two thought processes, cyclic and linear (Fig. 15) and operates on the principle that as we alter the forest from the soil surface upward we simultaneously alter the forest from the soil surface downward (Figs. 11, 12, 13, 16, and 21). We must also understand and accept that the variability within and among forest stages is infinite because the variability is composed of ever-changing small, short cycles within larger, longer cycles within larger, longer cycles, etc., and every cycle ultimately completes itself because time is a human construct

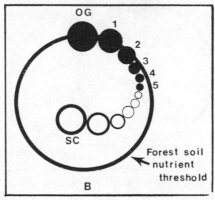

Fig. 29-B. The same principles are functioning here as in Fig. 29-A, but instead of letting the forest (solid circles) repair itself after the third (3) rotation, a fourth (4) and fifth (5) rotation are attempted. The soil nutrient capital is well into a deficit budget by the fourth rotation and is definitely irretrievable by the fifth rotation; the belowground, ecological processes are irretrievably altered by the fifth rotation and the forest community becomes a shrub community (open circles, SC) that may last decades to centuries, depending on the severity of management damage to the site. Note that intensive management brings the forest community to an earlier, simpler successional stage, shrub community—a predictable consequence of intensive product-oriented plantation management that reduces the forest soil nutrient capital into the deficit budget. The forest soil deficit budget, however, is a surplus budget for the shrub community, which over time can reestablish the maintenance budget for the gradual return of the forest community.

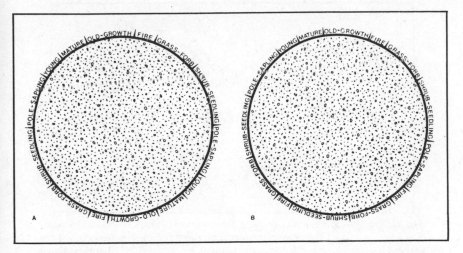

Fig. 30. The following scenarios are only two possibilities among infinite variation on any given site. In example A, classic forest succession takes place, but the length of time in each stage can vary from years to decades to centuries and depends on a myriad of conditions. In example B, fire starts succession over before the old-growth stage is reached; if fires are frequent enough, several centuries may pass before old-growth again occupies the site.

and not relevant to a forest (Fig. 30). Thus, restoration forestry is born in the concept of variable rotation ages based on both biological and product objectives through time that *simulate* Nature's blueprint over a landscape. We can also think of it as satellite forestry in that we use satellites to see the whole forest simultaneously so we can manage a changing mix of plantations and forests over a landscape in a way that simulates Nature's irregularity and allows every acre to become a forest often enough and long enough to be self-sustaining, self-repairing (Fig. 31).

Intensive plantation management is a child of short-term economics in which the entire focus is on fast-grown woodfiber, and anything diverted to another product is considered an economic failure. Such management is mutually exclusive of virtually all other human values because rigid constraints of time and a single-species monoculture define the plantation. Spotted owls, for example, cannot survive in a continuous 80-year-old plantation. Water quality and soil fertility are severely impaired with the cumulative effects of erosion—both chemical and physical, compaction, and the loss of soil organic matter, such as large woody

183

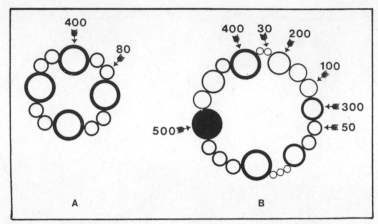

Fig. 31. This figure represents a forest/plantation management scheme for the same acres through time. The management scheme depicted in A represents 4 forest stages (400 year old) interspersed with 8 plantations (80 year old). Each plantation is used to maximize production of low-quality, fast-grown woodfiber, which rapidly draws on stored, soil nutrient reserves and impacts ecological processes—both aboveground and belowground—through management activities. Each forest stage allows soil nutrient capital to be replaced and ecological processes to be repaired; this is the time of reinvestment in the forest system in preparation for the next plantations. While the forest is repairing itself, high-quality, slowly grown woodfiber is being produced. The formula for this management scheme is f-p-p-f-p-p-f-p-p-f-p-f (f=forest, which is more than 100 years old; p = plantation, which is less than 100 years old) and takes 2,240 years to complete. Example B takes 3,050 years and shows the wide variation of options possible in woodfiber production while simultaneously producing other products and amenities, such as clean water and spotted owls.

debris. In addition, the human values of recreation and spiritual renewal are also missing. Restoration forestry, on the other hand, relaxes the constraints of time and a single-species monoculture on forest acres with the result that all values exist on some acres all of the time (Fig. 32). Whereas intensive plantation management is cost-deferred, short-term, single-product exploitation, restoration forestry is a pay-as-you-go sustainable forest that simultaneously produces a multitude of products and amenities over centuries.

One of the reasons we appear to have so much difficulty grasping long-term ideas, such as restoration forestry, is the brevity of our life. "If our lifetimes are so short how can we learn to manage such long-term forests?" is a question I am frequently asked. I can see several options, and I know there are others I don't see. One option

184

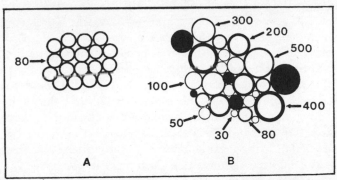

Fig. 32. The circles represent forest stands; open circles are managed stands and solid circles are living laboratories of unmanaged stands of various ages set aside from which to learn sustainable, restoration forestry. Numbers represent age at harvest of managed stands. A is plantation management in which age of harvest is all 80 years. Such plantation management is mutually exclusive of almost all human values except fast-grown woodfiber, and plantation management is not sustainable on a continual basis. B is restoration forestry. Note that plantation management for fast-grown woodfiber (stand ages 30–100 years) is a part of restoration forestry. When constraints of time and single-species monocultures are relaxed (stand ages 200–500 years), the forest can replenish its soil nutrient and process capital; the quality and quantity of ground water and streams and riparian zones are restored; spotted owl, pileated woodpecker, and marten habitats are recreated; and old-growth forest conditions are simulated for human recreation and spiritual renewal. Throughout this whole process—restoration of an ecologically functional forest—quality and quantity woodfiber is produced on a sustained basis for a diverse market, and public user fees and fee hunting and fishing can generate revenue annually prior to timber harvest.

is to form a small group of highly qualified forest scientists, managers, and an economist and send them around the world for a year or two to study special cases and common denominators of world forest practices and problems to figure out what works, what does not, and why. The USDA Soil Conservation Service learned much about soil erosion this way in the 1930's. Another option is to determine the most pressing ecological management problems today, then hire one highly skilled group of people per problem to gather all the literature and write a synthesis. This would be a thorough, integrated, up-to-date report of what we think we know and what we think we need to know. We could literally catapult ourselves forward in the knowledge of forests and forest management (or other management problems) if we did only these two things.

Simultaneously, of course, we can continue research, both the

185

usual short-term research and innovative long-term research, such as the 220-year study of decomposing logs in the H.J. Andrews Experimental Forest in the Cascade Range of western Oregon (Wyant 1986). Long-term research projects can also be designed and executed on public lands as a carefully monitored part of ongoing management practices. What we do today could be interpreted two, three, or more generations from now; this is the only way some critical answers will be derived. Still another approach to research is to consider Christmas tree farms as the simplest form of forest plantation management. We will learn much about the forest if we can make Christmas tree farms sustainable over time. By studying both ends of the forest—old-growth (the most complex) and Christmas tree farms (the most simple)—we should learn much about the hidden thresholds of forest processes that drive the system. Much research also needs to be done on the ecological sustainablity of young-growth forest plantations managed for woodfiber over one, two, or three short rotations.

We, in western Oregon, western Washington, and southwestern British Columbia have the richest conifer forest in the world and, as yet, the healthiest. We have a benign climate, clean air, clean water, and fertile soils; and we have had a severe impact on our forest only within the last century. The ecology of our forest is also better known than that of any other forest in the world. All this gives us the time, if we are committed and we begin now, to learn how to sustain a forest through restoration forestry (Photo 47). We have the only chance left in the world! Only when we have accomplished this, can we call ourselves "Foresters," and only then can we help the people of the world to restore the health of their watersheds, produce a sustainable variety of forest products, and also retain their other amenities.

Although I sometimes look down at Mother Earth from an airplane and all I can say is, "Please forgive us for we know not what we do," I see restoration forestry as a way to atone for our past. Restoration forestry will work because " . . . the very process of restoring the land to health is the process through which we become attuned with Nature and, through Nature, with ourselves. Restoration ecology, therefore, is both the means and the end, for as we learn how to restore the land, we heal the ecosystem, and as we heal the ecosystem, we heal ourselves. We also simultaneously restore both our options for products and amenities from the land and the options of future generations. This is crucial because our

Photo 47. Restoration forestry is possible. It encompasses all age-classes of plantations while maintaining carefully and well distributed stands of Nature's old-growth, mid-aged, and young-growth trees from which to learn how to sustain the forest. (Photograph by author.)

moral obligation as human beings is to maintain options for future generations (Maser 1988a).

As Han Solo said in the movie "The Empire Strikes Back," "Don't ever tell me the odds," which means we're only *limited* by what *we think we can't do*. It isn't that we don't know enough to grow sustainable forests. We simply have chosen not to. The choice is ours. The consequences are ours and the future's (Maser 1988b).

## The future is today

As I said in the preface, if we dare to dream boldly enough, we can have a sustainable forest in the Pacific Northwest that includes old-growth trees, and woodfiber, and wilderness, and elk, and native trout, and clean water, and, and. . . . But like the Old West movies, we'll have to check our guns at the door; we will have to change our thinking, our view of the forest; and we will have to transcend our own special interests and encompass all interests in the forest as a whole. To do this, to change our thinking, we will have to accept that we, as product-consuming humans, are the problem, so we are also the *solution.*

I recently was the speaker at the annual banquet of a conservation organization, and I spoke about a dream large enough to encompass the various interests of people in a sustainable forest in a way that maintains and nurtures human dignity. When I was finished, two young men questioned my honesty and my faith in humanity. They both steadfastly insisted that there had to be enemies out there to hate, and I was dishonest if I didn't agree. Bennett (1987), in a newspaper article, quoted John Stockwell, an ex-Central Intelligence Agency (CIA) employee, as saying that "American foreign policy [is] a result of [a] need for enemies." I can only see two possible reasons for "needing" an enemy. The first is to have a person onto whom I can project my fear and thereby feel more in control internally. The second is the illusion that if I project my fear onto an "enemy" I am absolved of all responsibility for my thoughts and actions. I do not see people as enemies, however; I see them as candles. And a candle loses nothing of its light by lighting another candle.

Another consideration is the power of an idea. An idea that is acted upon can change the world. Look, for example, to the Middle East where Judaism, Christianity, and Islam, each attributed to a separate individual, all arose in an area about the size of western Oregon. The growth of these ideas into religions, each in its turn, changed the world. There is a lesson in this: if you want to own "your idea," to get credit for it, then keep it to yourself and it will change nothing. If, on the other hand, you want an idea to effect change, you must give it away freely so everyone who wishes to may own it. Even if you don't care who gets credit for "your idea," you must remember that large organizations and societies change with glacial speed.

Still another consideration is change. There is much insistence today that either we need not change because science and technology will give us the answer or that we dare not change until science and technology gives us the answer. Keep in mind that science, with the aid of technology, can tell us what happens, why it happens, how it happens, where it happens, how much it happens, and perhaps even what we need to do to alter a predicted outcome. But science cannot change it for us; we the people must figure out how to do that. Put differently, scientific data without a context—*the dream*—in which to frame it is like a jigsaw puzzle without pattern and border. To change anything in a meaningful sense, we must first know what is there, then we must decide what we want to be there, and then we must figure out what the options are to achieve that which we desire. As stated in "Alice in Objectiveland," we must struggle with defining our objectives. I can, for instance, define "sustainable forest" for you, but then it is my definition—not yours. For the Pacific Northwest to be managed on the basis of a sustainable forest, we must struggle with the definition together so we can all "own" the outcome—that means all of us: people from public land management agencies, industrialists, conservationists, and anyone else interested in the forest. We the people must define our dream and choose to strive for it.

Our forests are certain to decline through time with present management attitudes and practices. Once our dream is defined, however, and the choice is made to pursue it, we not only have the chance to achieve it but also the flexibility to see and take advantage of heretofore unseen options. To have a sustainable forest, we must maintain some unmanaged old-growth, midaged-growth, and young-growth forest stands from which to learn. If we are willing to maintain these unmanaged stands, we suddenly have flexibility we didn't have before. For example, if we cut all the old-growth simply to maintain the present volume of woodfiber for industry, society will be jolted suddenly when the old-growth is gone and jobs with it, and we'll lose all the potential options old-growth afforded. On the other hand, if we have saved enough of the unmanaged stands from which to learn how to sustain a forest, then industrial changes can be gradual, minimizing costly court battles, and the human transition can be made with dignity and as gently as possible, perhaps over 20 to 30 years. In addition, old-growth stands have recently revealed, through their fire history (Morrison and Swanson, in press), that they often are similar to selective logged forests that have been maintained over time while products have simultaneously been removed, another option for future management of long rotations in a sustainable forest.

Our dream—a sustainable forest—must be bold enough to allow change not only in the forest but also in our thinking because the land is not to be conquered but is to be nurtured. We must also understand, accept, and remember that the world is always in a state of becoming, in a state of change, so nothing is ever "finished." Thus, if we try to hold things constant, like yesterday's timber values projected into tomorrow's forests, then it is like driving through life looking in the rearview mirror. Today's decisions will design and sustain or destroy the forests of tomorrow.

We, the people of the United States, are like a great American quilt. We too often pursue our science and our technology in intellectual isolation of their long-term consequences to the environment. Our science and our technology are like the isolated pieces of a great, patchwork quilt with a largely random arrangement and without a thread to either relate the pieces one to the other or to hold them together. Native Americans, on the other hand, have the thread; it is a deep spiritual relatedness to the land. If we are to have a sustainable environment for ourselves and our children, we must adopt the Native American values of relatedness to the land and apply them to our values of science and technology. Thus, as we the people elevate our personal, environmental and social consciousness, the constant human struggle, we begin to take our rightful place in the universe—not as conquerors, for we have conquered nothing, but as universal custodians. In this way we can both design our quilt and sew it together for all generations to enjoy.

If *we the people* really want a sustainable forest in the Pacific Northwest, then Mortimer J. Adler has a thought for us, ". . . The government of the United States is not in Washington, not in the White House, not in the Capitol . . . the government of the United States resides in us, *we the people* [emphasis mine]. What resides in Washington is the *administration* [emphasis mine] of our government." We, individually and collectively, must therefore constantly be willing to risk change if we are to grow enough to envision and maintain a sustainable forest because life, after all, is a matter of faith, not of sight. Time is of the essence. We have to start *NOW* because we are simultaneously the hope and the limitation of the future. Neil Postman said that, "Children are the living messages we send to a time we will not see." What shall we send with them into that distant time—hope or the drums of fear?

# APPENDIX 1

## COMMON AND SCIENTIFIC NAMES

| COMMON NAME | SCIENTIFIC NAME |
|---|---|
| **FUNGI:** | |
| Blackstain root rot | *Verticicladiella wageneri* |
| Laminate root rot | *Phellinus weiri* |
| Red ring rot | *Phellinus pini* |
| | |
| **PLANTS:** | |
| Alaska-yellow cedar | *Chamaecyparis nootkatensis* |
| Alder | *Alnus* spp. |
| Beech | *Fagus* spp. |
| Birch | *Betula* spp. |
| Coast redwood | *Sequoia sempervirens* |
| Common hornbeam | *Carpinus betulus* |
| Douglas fir | *Pseudotsuga menziesii* |
| Elm | *Ulmus* spp. |
| Engelmann spruce | *Picea engelmannii* |
| European beech | *Fagus sylvatica* |
| Fir | *Abies* spp. |
| Hemlock | *Tsuga* spp. |
| Hickory | *Carya* spp. |
| Incense-cedar | *Libocedrus decurrens* |
| Larch | *Larix* spp. |
| Linden | *Tilia* spp. |
| Mountain hemlock | *Tsuga mertensiana* |
| Noble fir | *Abies procera* |
| Norway spruce | *Picea abies* |
| Oak | *Quercus* spp. |
| Pine | *Pinus* spp. |

| | |
|---|---|
| Ponderosa pine | *Pinus ponderosa* |
| Port-Orford cedar | *Chamaecyparis lawsoniana* |
| Scotch pine | *Pinus sylvestris* |
| Silver fir | *Abies amabilis* |
| Sitka spruce | *Picea sitchensis* |
| Spruce | *Picea* spp. |
| Sugar pine | *Pinus lambertiana* |
| Sycamore | *Plantanus* spp. |
| Western hemlock | *Tsuga heterophylla* |
| Western larch | *Larix occidentalis* |
| Western redcedar | *Thuja* plicata |
| Western white pine | *Pinus monticola* |

INVERTEBRATES:

| | |
|---|---|
| Carpenter ant | *Camponotus* spp. |
| Douglas fir tussock moth | *Orgyia pseudotsugata* |
| Gribble | *Limnoria* spp. |
| Western spruce budworm | *Choristoneura fumiferana* |
| (2 species) | *Choristoneura occidentalis* |

BIRDS:

| | |
|---|---|
| Horned lark | *Eremophila alpestris* |
| Pileated woodpecker | *Dryocopus pileatus* |
| Sage grouse | *Centrocercus urophasianus* |
| Spotted owl | *Strix occidentalis* |

MAMMALS:

| | |
|---|---|
| Black bear | *Ursus americanus* |
| Deer | *Odocoileus hemionus* |
| Deer mouse | *Peromyscus maniculatus* |
| Ground squirrels | *Spermophilus* spp. |
| Northern flying squirrel | *Glaucomys sabrinus* |

# APPENDIX 2

*Footnote 3*

In various historical periods, economic activity has sought to displace the forests from the fertile coastlands in favor of agriculture, and at the same time the stock farmers everywhere have destroyed the high forest. . . . [Those] that survive to the present are located in the mountains, especially the remote, spacious Pindus. In the isolated but easily accessible mountain ranges of the southern Peloponnesus, of Parnassus and Olympus, the areas of forest have shrunken severely.

In Homeric times, Greece was, of course, much more heavily forested. Homer describes as wooded islands Samos and Zakynthos, which today are largely cleared and treeless. The mountains supported a rich fauna, with lions, deer, and boars; here the Homeric heroes disported themselves in the hunt. "Deep," "endless," "shadowy," indeed "virgin," Homer calls these stands of trees, and even in the area of cultivated land the temple precincts were left in the shadows of holy groves.

Certainly, utilization of the woodlands had begun. Woodcutters entered the forests with their axes to obtain material for shipbuilding and house construction. Wood was needed for fortifications, for illumination, and for the hearthfire. Shepherds drove their flocks into the stands of trees, especially prizing the acorn mast. Still more brutally, windstorms and catastrophic wildfires threatened those "endless," those "virgin" forest areas of the Eighth and Seventh Centuries B.C. Often shepherds may have set these fires, but in the summer period of dryness they also were ignited by lightning. Frequently, it was possible for nature to repair these losses with the help of pioneer tree species, as for example the reproduction of the Aleppo pine. But when the shepherds returned again and again to the same forest stands with fire, axe, and grazing flocks, soil erosion ensued, and with this the high forest gradually disappeared. . . .

In the history of the most famous Greek city, Athens, the fact that wood shortage is a result of deforestation is made very clear. The land of Athens and also the offshore Aegean archipelago lie in the rain-shadow of great mountain ranges and experience an especially long dry period in the summer. The available forests of stone oak and Aleppo pine in the foothills had to serve numerous requirements of the country and city economy of Attica, as meager pasture for goats and sheep, as sources of charcoal for industrial and domestic fuel, of vine supports in the vineyards, of pit props in the silver mines. So the environs of Athens became forest-poor in early times.

In the Persian Wars[,] Athens grew into a sea power and required ship-building timber from that time on, a resource which the hinterland of the city hardly provided. So the Athenian Empire got caught in a serious dependence on its timber suppliers, primarily on the mountainous kingdom of Macedonia in the north. In order to secure this supply, the city founded the colony of Amphipolis in 436 B.C. at the mouth of the River Strymon. But when the Peloponnesian War broke out between Athens and Sparta, Sparta blockaded the timber supply to Attica by besieging Amphipolis. "This caused the Athenians no small trouble," says the historian Thucydides, an eyewitness. In the later years of the war the Spartan party also succeeded in destroying a timber depot of the Athenians in Italy and, on their own side, in obtaining ship-building timber from Mt. Ida in Asia Minor through the aid of the Persian administration there. Since the Spartans at the same time controlled the timber supplies of the Greek and Macedonian high mountains, the Athenian authorities finally were unable to build another fleet, and lost their position as paramount power in Greece to Sparta by their capitulation in 404.

The cause-and-effect relationship between deforestation and timber shortage must have made a deep impression on the defeated city-state; at any rate Plato expressed himself eloquently on this subject in one of his later political writings. In the dialogue *Critias* he described the landscape of Attica in the Golden Age:

In what respect may this present land justly be called a remnant of what once existed? In that the earth, where it was once soft and rich, has washed away everywhere, and only the bare skeleton of the land has been left behind . . . But then (in early times) the mountains were highand covered with soil, and likewise the plains, which now have come to be called stony fields, were full of rich earth; furthermore the mountains bore thick forests, of which visible evidence survives to the present day. For there are some mountains which now offer only food for bees, but not long ago trees were felled there for rafters in the largest buildings, the roofs of which still stand intact . . . Furthermore, the land enjoyed an annual rainfall from Zeus which was not lost to it, as now, when it quickly flows off from the thin, unreceptive ground into the sea; but the soil it then had was rich and deep, so the rain soaked into it and was stored up in the retentive loamy soil (Rubner 1985, pp. 778 and 780).

*Footnote 4*

. . . The calculations made 150 years ago without our modern knowledge and the help of yield tables, site maps, and so on proved to be exact in one regard. . . . The economic superiority of the softwoods over the hardwoods is an indisputable fact.

The biological consequences are less pleasant. *It took about one century for them to show up clearly* [emphasis mine]. Many of the pure stands grew excellently in the first generation but already showed an amazing retrogression in the second generation. The reason for this is a very complex one and only a simplified explanation can be given. A spruce stand may serve as an example. Our spruce roots are normally very shallow. Planted on former hardwood soil, the spruce roots could follow the deep root channels of the former hardwoods in the first generation. But in the second generation the root systems turned shallow on account of progressive soil compaction. As a result, the available nutrient supply for the trees became smaller. The spruce stand could profit from mild humus accumulated in the first genera- tion by the hardwoods, but it was not able to produce a mild humus itself. Spruce litter rots much more slowly than broadleaf litter and is much more difficult for the fauna and flora of the upper soil layer to decompose. Therefore, a raw humus developed in most cases. Its humic acids started to leach the soil under our humid climate and impoverished the soil fauna and

197

flora. This caused an even poorer decomposition and a faster development of raw humus. Then the whole nutrient cycle got out of order and eventually was nearly stopped. The nutrient accumulation in raw humus cannot be used easily. The soluble nutrients of the upper soil layer were washed down, and the spruce roots could not reach that far. This development in its extreme can lead to the formation of a bog. Anyway, *the drop of one or even two or more site classes during two or three generations of pure spruce is a well known and frequently observed fact. This represents a production loss of 20 to 30 percent* [emphasis mine]. The reactions of the soil to pure pine stands are similar to those of spruce in many ways. These experiences can follow in pure plantations within and beyond the natural distribution area if one does not include the subalpine spruce region in this consideration. But generally one can say the farther out of its natural distribution a species is cultivated, the worse it becomes (Plochmann 1968, pp. 24 and 25).

*Footnote 5*

As stated in the Office of Technology Assessment report "Watershed-related Technologies for Sustainable Agriculture in U.S. Arid/Semiarid Lands" (Kendrick et al. 1983, page 10), under "Watershed Management":

> Two major classes of watersheds occur in the Western United States: 1) highland watersheds, located in the major mountain ranges and consisting of the untimbered "alpine" zone (above the timberline) and the timbered "montane" zone; and 2) lowland watersheds consisting of grass- or brush-covered valleys and plains. Watershed-management technologies are designed to increase surface runoff by vegetation removal or replacement or by other surface modifications.
>
> No proven technologies exist to increase water yield from the alpine zone. This area may be the most efficient and productive source of water in the Western United States, and a passive, conservative management approach may be the most beneficial and effective management technology at present for downstream users.
>
> In certain situations in the montane zone, vegetation management through timber harvesting may produce local increases in water yield. It may be difficult, however, to detect increased yields at points downstream where arid/semiarid agriculture is practiced because such increases, when combined with the entire

volume of watershed runoff may not be discernible using existing stream-gage technologies. Moreover, the ability to predict results of application on an unstudied watershed is difficult because of the range of hydrologic environments in the mountains of the West relative to that represented by existing experimental results. At some sites the effects of timber harvest on soil erosion, other components of the hydrologic cycle, or existing wilderness values may negate potential beneficial effects for downstream arid/semiarid agriculture.

Results of attempts to produce additional surface runoff from lowland watersheds have been varied because of the natural hydrologic variability of the lowland watersheds and the range of purpose of the technologies. Because practices are very site-specific, they have more local than regional significance. In most cases where the dominant vegetation consists of shrubs and grasses, management should emphasize forage production and erosion prevention rather than surface runoff production. Where surface runoff is collected and used for cultivated crops and animal watering (runoff agriculture), water- management practices can provide an important local water supply.

*Footnote 6*

As stated in the Office of Technology Assessment report *Water-related Technologies for Sustainable Agriculture in U.S. Arid/Semiarid Lands* (Kendrick et al. 1983, pp. 6 and 7), under "Watershed Management":

Available estimates of water supply and use indicate that *almost half of the Western United States is experiencing water-supply problems in relation to demand* [emphasis mine]. Surface water shortages exist annually or seasonally in at least some portion of each of the major water resources regions of the Western States. In almost all cases, these shortages are offset by water reuse and ground water pumping. In much of the Southwest and southern High Plains, ground water is being withdrawn laster than it is replace (often called ground water 'mining') in order to sustain developed levels of use. Where water supply is not being consumed, competing nonconsumptive uses, such as instream flow requirements for hydroelectric generation, waste assimilation, recreation, and habitat maintenance, increasingly create scheduling conflicts for offstream uses. . . . *Present trends and experience indicate that every additional drop of water conserved, and thus available, enables more growth and development, raising demand levels further. Effective water-use management will necessitate attention to demand as well as supply aspects of water use* [emphasis mine].

The availability of water for agricultural use varies by location and over time. Water supply depends on variations in components of the hydrologic cycle—precipitation, evaporation, transpiration, infiltration, and runoff. *Because these components interrelate, a change produced by technology in one component of the cycle will inevitably affect other components* [emphasis mine].

The potential for a given technology to produce additional water or to conserve existing supplies is difficult to evaluate and will remain so unless the quantities of water involved in the hydrologic cycle can be defined more accurately. Various responsibilities for the collection, synthesis, and dissemination of hydrologic information are delegated among a number of Federal and State agencies . . . resulting in a variety of data bases and data interpretations that are often not compatible. Important gaps in data exist, and few regional syntheses of data have been made. *Short-term climatic fluctuations affecting water supply can be accommodated in management and planning processes through statistical analysis of past trends; there is no reliable method for predicting long-term fluctuations* [emphasis mine].

The most important source of renewable surface water supplies in the Western United States is the mountain snowpack. When the snowpack melts in the spring and summer, it supplies an estimated 70 to 100 percent (depending on location) of the total annual surface runoff for all river basins except the Texas-Gulf region. Relatively little research attention has been given to the snowpack. Technologies such as weather modification and the forecasting of streamflow to improve reservoir management would benefit considerably from increased understanding of the snowpack's dominant role in renewing surface water supplies.

And finally, the introductory paragraph of the report states (p. 3):

As a Nation with bountiful resources, the United States has rarely faced natural resource limits. *In the short history of this country, there have always been more lands and more resources to develop and a philosophy that technology could supplement natural resources when needed* [emphasis mine]. Increasingly, however, some Western States are experiencing resource limitations related to water use and distribution that challenge the full capacity of existing social and technical institutions. The water problems to face this region and, therefore, the Nation in the 1980's and 1990's are likely to expand and intensify for agriculture. *Stretching resources to accommodate the West's continuing growth while protecting existing patterns of water demand may require levels of technical input no longer*

200

*economically feasible* [emphasis mine]. Concerted Federal, State, and local action will be needed to help build a sustainable Western agriculture that is profitable for the Western farmer and rancher and that effectively addresses the complex and interrelated problems surrounding the agricultural use of Western water. A strong Federal role will remain fundamental to help bring about necessary changes.

# LITERATURE CITED

Allen, G.M. and Gould, E.M., Jr. 1986. Complexity, wickedness, and public forests. J. For. 84:20–23.

Anonymous. 1985. Poland courting ecological disaster. The Daily Barometer, Oreg. State Univ., Corvallis, 10 December.

Anonymous. 1986a. The Millennium Grove massacre. The Daily Barometer, Oreg. State Univ., Corvallis, 7 April.

Anonymous. 1986b. Both camps unhappy with spotted owl decision. The Oregonian, Portland, OR. 8 August.

Anonymous. 1986c. Life disrupted: Rhine went wrong. Corvallis Gazette-Times, Corvallis, OR. 15 November.

Anonymous. 1986d. Water quality new farm problem. The Daily Barometer, Oreg. State Univ., Corvallis, 22 April.

Anonymous. 1986e. Mill modernization will cost 60 jobs. Corvallis Gazette-Times, Corvallis, OR. 16 February.

Anonymous. 1986f. Ravage in the rain forests. U.S. News & World Report, 31 March:61–62.

Anonymous. 1986g. Floods, cancer seen if ozone loss unchecked. Corvallis Gazette-Times, Corvallis, OR. 11 June.

Anonymous. 1986h. Nepal tree-planting fight provokes new scrutiny. Corvallis Gazette-Times, Corvallis, OR. 6 June.

Anonymous. 1987a. Chernobyl fallout may destroy Lapp's way of life. The Daily Barometer, Oreg. State Univ., Corvallis, 16 February.

Anonymous. 1987b. Scientists say we've lost war with insects. The Daily Barometer, Oreg. State Univ., Corvallis, 19 February.

Anonymous. 1987c. Scientists warn tropical forest face destruction. Corvallis Gazette-Times, Corvallis, OR. 24 April.

Baden, J. 1987. Alaska timber policies fiscally, morally bankrupt. The Oregonian, Portland, OR. 11 March.

Baker, D. 1986. Virgin forests under fire. Natl. Wildl. 24:4–10.

Barsh, R.L. 1979. The Washington fishing rights controversy: an economic critique. (Rev. ed.). Graduate School of Business Administration, Univ. of Wash., Seattle, 128 pp.

Bella, D.A. 1987a. Organizations and systematic distortion of information. J. Profl Issues in Engrg. 113:360–370.

Bella, D.A. 1987b. Engineering and the erosion of trust. J. Profl Issues in Engrg. 113:117–129.

Bella, D.A. and W.S. Overton 1972. Environmental planning and ecological possibilities. J. Sanitary Engrg. Div. ASCE 98:579–592.

Bella, D.A., C.D. Mosher, and S.N. Calvo. 1988a. Technocracy and trust: Nuclear waste controversy. J. Profl. Issues in Engrg. 114:27–39.

Bella, D.A., C.D. Mosher, and S.N. Calvo. 1988b. Establishing trust: Nuclear waste disposal. J. Profl. Issues in Engrg. 114:40–50.

Bennett, T. 1987. American foreign policy a result of need for enemies, Stockwell says. The Daily Barometer, Oreg. State Univ., Corvallis, 28 May.

Bernier, B. and Winget, C.H. (Eds). Proc. Fourth N. Amer. Soils Conf., Les Presses de L'Université Laval, Québec, Canada.

Blaschke, H. and Bäumler, W. 1986. Über die Rolle der Biogeozönose im Wurzelbereich von Waldbäumen. Forstwissenschaft. Centralb. 2:122–130.

Blumm, M.C. 1987. Fewer roads fast way to improve elk habitat. The Oregonian, Portland, OR. 10 June.

BML (Bundesministerium fur Ernahrung, Landwirtschaft und forsten, ed.). 1976. Wald, forst-und Holzwirtshaft, Jagd in der Bundesrepublik Deutschland, AID, Munster-Hiltrup. 184 pp.

Botkin, D.B. 1979. A grandfather clock down the staircase: stability and disturbance in natural ecosystems. pp. 1–10. In: Forests: Fresh Perspectives from Ecosystem Analysis. Waring, R.H. (Ed.). Proc. 40th Ann. Biol. Colloquium, Ore. State Univ. Press, Corvallis.

Brauns, A. 1955. Applied soil biology and plant protection. pp. 231–240. In: Soil zoology. D.K. McE. Kevan (Ed.). Butterworths, London.

Brown, L.R. 1981. World population growth, soil erosion, and food security. Science 214:995–1002.

Bruck, R.I., Robarge, W.P. 1984. Observations of boreal montane forest decline in the southern Appalachian Mountains: soil and vegetation studies. In: Aquatic effects task group (E) and terrestrial effects task group (F) research summaries. North Carolina State Acid Deposition Program. Raleigh, 425 pp.

Bukkyo Dendo Kyokai. 1985. The teaching of Buddha. (One hundred & tenth revised edition). Kosaido Printing Co., Ltd., Tokyo, Japan. 307 pp.

Butzer, K.W. 1961. Climatic change in arid regions since the Pliocene;. In A history of land use in arid regions. UNESCO, Paris, France.

Butzke, H. 1984. Untersuchungsergebnisse aus Waldböden Nordrhein-Westfalens zur Frage der Bodenversauerung durch Immissionen. Wissenschaft und Umwelt. 2:80–88.

Cain, M.D. and Yaussy, D.A. 1984. Can hardwoods be eradicated from pine sites? South. J. Applied For. 8:7–12.

Capra, F. 1975. The Tao of physics. Shambhala, Berkeley, CA. 330 pp.

Carroll, L. 1933. Alice's adventures in wonderland. Doubleday, Doran, & Co., New York, NY. 162 pp.

Carter, V.G. and Dale, T. 1974. Topsoil and civilization (Rev. Ed.). Univ. Oklahoma Press, Norman. 292 pp.

Chasan, D.J. 1977. Up for grabs, inquiries into who wants what. Madrona Publ., Inc., Seattle, WA 133 pp.

Corvallis Gazette-Time's View. 1986. Lumber barons use owls for scapegoats. Corvallis Gazette-Times, Corvallis, OR. 13 August.

Cousins, N. 1975. The fatalists versus the doers. J. For. 73:103–104, 112.

Cramer, H.H. 1984. On the predisposition to disorders of middle European forests. Pflanzenschutz-Nachrichten. 37:98–207.

Cramer, H.H. and Cramer-Middendorf, M. 1984. Studies on the relationships between periods of damage and factors of climate in the middle Europeanforests since 1851. Pflanzenschutz-Nachrichten. 37:208–334.

Crosson, P. 1979. Agricultural land use: A technological and energy perspective. pp. 99–111. In: Schnepf, M. (Ed.). Farmland food and the Future. Soil Conserv. Serv. of Amer., Ankeny, IA.

Crowell, J.B., Jr. 1986. More, not less, timber should be cut. The Oregonian, Portland, OR., 11 June 1986.

Cox, T.R., Maxwell, R.S., Thomas, P.D., Malone, J.J. 1985. This well-wood land, Americans and their forests from colonial times to the present. Univ. Nebraska Press, Lincoln. 325 pp.

Dean, W. 1985. Forest conservation in southeastern Brazil, 1900–1955. Environ. Rev. 9:54–69.

DeLoach, C.J. 1971. The effect of habitat diversity on predation. Proc. Tall Timbers Conf. on Ecol. Anim. Control by Habitat Manage. 2:223–241.

DeYonge, J. 1985. Who-o-o-o cares about old forests, owls pit naturalists vs. loggers. The Seattle Times/Seattle Post-Intelligencer, Seattle, WA. 8 December.

Deumling, D. 1986. Acid rain just incorrect name. The Oregonian, Portland, OR., 19 September.

Dunne, T. and Leopold, L.B. 1978. Water in environmental planning. W.H. Freeman and Co., San Francisco, CA. 818 pp.

Easwaran, E. 1986. The thousand names of the Lord. The Little Lamp. 26:109–147.

Ehrlich, P.R. 1985. Humankind's war against Homo Sapiens. Defenders. 60:4–12.

Eiseley, L. 1973. The man who saw through time. Charles Scribner's Sons, New York, NY. 125 pp.

Evans, B. 1986. Forest giants falling fast. Audubon Action. 4–10.

Fisher, R., Melham, T. Ramsay, C.R., Stuart, G.S. 1986. Nature on the rampage, our violent earth. National Geographic Society, Washington, D.C. 199 pp.

Fogel, R. and Trappe, J.M. 1978. Fungus consumption (mycophagy) by small animals. Northw. Sci. 52:1–31.

Forsman, E.D., Meslow, E.C., and Wight, H.M. 1984. Distribution and biology of the spotted owl in Oregon. Wildl. Monogr. 87:1–64.

Foundation For Inner Peace. 1975. A course in miracles, Vol. 2, Workbook for students. Found. For Inner Peace, Tiburon, CA. 478 pp.

Foundation For Inner Peace. 1975. A course in miracles, Vol. 3, Manual for teachers. Found. For Inner Peace, Tiburon, CA. 88 pp.

Forrester, S. 1986. The invisible shadow in the forests. Register Guard, Eugene, OR. 8 June.

Frankl, V. E. 1963. Man's search for meaning. Beacon Press, New York, NY. 237 pp.

Franklin, J.F. In press. Structural and functional diversity in temperate forests. In: Proceedings of the Smithsonian-National Academy of Sciences Forum on BioDiversity. Natl. Acad. Press, Wash., D.C.

Franklin, J.F., Cromack, K., Jr., Denison, W., McKee, A., Maser, C., Sedell, J., Swanson, F., and Juday, G. 1981. Ecological characteristics of old-growth Douglas-fir forests. USDA For. Serv. Gen. Tech. Rep. PNW-118, 48 pp. Pac. Northwest Forest and Range Exp. Stn., Portland, OR.

Franklin, J.F., Hall, F., Laudenslayer, W., Maser, C., Nunan, J., Poppino, J., Ralph, C.J., Spies, T. 1986. Interim definitions for old-growth Douglas-fir and mixed-conifer forests in the Pacific Northwest and California. USDA For. Serv. Res. Note PNW-447, 7 p. Pac. Northwest Forest and Res. Exp. Stn., Portland, OR.

Franklin, J.F. and Spies, T.A. 1984. Characteristics of old-growth Douglas-fir forests. pp. 328–334. In: New forests for a changing world. Proc. Soc. of Amer. For. Natl. conf., Bethesda, MD.

Franz, H. and Loub, W. 1959. Bodenbiologische Untersuchungen an Walddüngungsuersuchen. Centralbl. Gesamte. Forstwes. 76:129–162.

Freud, S. 1961. The future of an illusion. W.W. Norton & Co., New York, NY. 63 pp.

Fries, N. 1966. Chemical factors in the germination of spores of Basidiomycetes. pp. 189–199. In: Madelin, M.F. (Ed.), The fungus spore. Butterworths, London.

Fries, N. 1982. Effects of plant roots and growing mycelia on Basidiospore germination in mycorrhiza-forming fungi. pp. 493–508. In: Laursen, G.A. and Ammirati, J.F. (Ed.). Arctic and alpine mycology. Univ. of Wash. Press, Seattle.

Giono, J. 1967. The man who planted hope and grew happiness. Friends of Nature, Brooksville, ME. 15 pp.

Goeller, D. 1986. Southern pine forest decline worrisome. The Oregonian, Portland, OR., 14 January.

Gronwall, O. and Pehrson, A. 1984. Nutrient content in fungi as a primary food of the red-squirrel Sciurus vulgaris L. Oecologia, 64:230–231.

Haines, W. 1986. Acid rain not the, or not the only, villain. The Oregonian, Portland, OR. 8 August.

Hall, E.R. 1981. The mammals of North America. Vol. 1 (2d ed.). John Wiley and Sons, NY. 600 pp.

Harley, J.L. and Smith, S.E. 1983. Mycorrhizal symbiosis. Academic Press, New York. NY. 483 pp.

Harmon, M.E., Franklin, J.F., Swanson, F.J., Sollins, P., Goregory, S.V., Lattin, J.D., Anderson, N.H., Cline, S.P., Sumen, N.G., Sedell, J.R., Lienkaemper, G.W., Cromack, K., Jr., Cummins, K.W. 1986. Ecology of coarse woody debris in temperate ecosystems. Advances in Ecological Research, Academic Press, New York, NY. 15:133–302.

Harris, J.M. 1981. Effect of rapid growth on wood processing. pp. 117–125. In: Proc., Div. 5, 17th IUFRO World Congress, Japan.

Harris, L.D. 1984. The fragmented forest. Univ. Chicago Press, Chicago, IL. 211 pp.

Harris, L.D. and Maser, C. 1984. Animal community characteristics. pp. 44–68. In: The fragmented forest. L.D. Harris. Univ. Chicago Press, Chicago, IL.

Harris, L.D., Maser, C., and McKee, A. 1982. Patterns of old-growth harvest and implications for Cascade wildlife. Trans. N. Amer. Wildl. Nat. Resour. Conf. 47:374–392.

Hesse, H. 1971. Siddhartha. Bantom Books, New York, NY. 152 pp.

Highsmith, R.M., Jr. and Kimerling, A.J. (Eds). 1979. Atlas of the Pacific Northwest (6th Ed.). Oreg. State Univ. Press, Corvallis, 135 pp.

Hill, S.B., Metz, L.J., and Farrier, M.H. 1975. Soil mesofauna and silvicultural practices. pp. 119–135. In: Forest soils and forest land management. Bernier, B. and Winget, C.H. (Eds). Proc. Fourth N. Amer. Soils Conf., Les Presses de L'Université Laval, Québec, Canada.

Hopwood, A., F. Marshall, and D. Smith. 1988. A case study: Discipline, ethics and the forestry profession in British Columbia. For. Plan. Can. 4:15–23.

Hyatt, C. and L. Gottlieb. 1987. When smart people fail. Simon and Schuster, Inc., New York, NY. 240 pp.

Hummel, F.C. 1985. The use of forests as a source of biomass energy. pp. 90–98. In: Proceedings of the Third International Conference on Energy from Biomass. Palz, W., Coombs, J., Hall, D.W. (Eds.). Elsevier Applied Sci. Publ., London, England.

Irwin, L. 1986. Ecology of the spotted owl in Oregon and Washington. National Council of the Paper Industry for Air and Stream Improvement, Inc. (NCASI), Tech. Bull. No. 509. 129 pp.

Jablanczy, A. 1988. Sustainable silviculture. For. Plan. Can. 4:7–9.

Jones, S. 1986. Fighting for trees. Corvallis Gazette-Times, Corvallis, OR. 27 July.

Jones, S. 1986. Slash burning blamed for hike in sea carcinogens. Corvallis Gazette-Times, Corvallis, OR. 25 April.

Jung, C.G. 1958. The undiscovered self. A Mentor Book, New York, NY. 125 pp.

Kadera, J. 1986a. Logging peril to spotted owl said listed in federal report. The Oregonian, Portland, OR. 1 August.

Kadera, J. 1986b. Spotted owl set-asides may wipe out 1,300 jobs. The Oregonian, Portland, OR. 8 August.

Kelly, D. and Braasch, G. 1986. The decadent forest. Audubon. 88:46–73.

Kendrick, J.B., Jr. (Chairman), Adams, A.A., Jr., Bahr, T.G., Blackburn, W.H., Dishman, W.T., Dregne, H.E., Evans, C.E., Gordon, L.J., Hagan, R.M., Herrick, D.E., Ingram, H., McKell, C., McNulty, M.F., Medelburg, M.E., Murino, C.J., Parker, A., Reed, C., Torres, L., Westfall, C.E., Jr., Whittlesey, N.K. 1983. Water-related technologies for sustainable agriculture in U.S. arid/semiarid lands. Off. Tech. Assess. U.S. Congress, U.S. Gov. Print. Off., Wash., D.C. OTA-F-212. 412 pp.

Kennedy, J.F. 1961. Profiles in courage. Harper & Row, New York, NY. 266 pp.

Kennedy, J.J. 1984. Understanding professional career evolution—an example of Aldo Leopold. Wildl. Soc. Bull. 12:215–226.

Knight, H.A. 1987. The pine decline. J. For. 85:25–28.

Kotter, M.M. and Farentinos, R.C. 1984. Formation of ponderosa pine ectomycorrhizae after inoculation with feces of tassel-eared squirrels. Mycologia, 76:758–760.

Kübler-Ross, E. 1969. On death and dying. Macmillan Publ. Co., Inc., New York, NY. 289 pp.

Lathem, E.C. (Ed.). 1969. The poetry of Robert Frost. Holt, Rinehart and Winston, Inc. New York, NY. 607 pp.

Leckenby, D.A., Sheehy, D.P., Nellis, C.H., Scherzinger, R.J., Luman, I.D., Elmore, W., Lemos, J.C., Doughty, L., Trainer, C.E. 1982. Mule deer. In: Wildlife habitats in managed rangelands—the Great Basin of southeastern Oregon. Thomas, J.W. and Maser, C. (Tech. Eds.). USDA For. Serv. GTR. PNW-139. 40 pp. Pac. Northwest For. and Range Exp. Sta., Portland, OR.

Lee, C.E., Martin, P., McCauley, J.R., O'Neill, T., Ramsay, C.R. 1986. Our awesome earth: Its mysteries and its splendors. Nat. Geogr. Soc., Wash., D.C. 199 pp.

Leopold, A. 1966. A sand county almanac, with other essays on conservation from Round River. Oxford Univ. Press, NY. 269 pp.

Li, C.Y. and Castellano, M.A. 1985. Nitrogen-fixing bacteria isolated from within sporocarps of three ectomycorrhizal fungi. p. 164. In: Molina, R. (Ed.), Proceedings 6th North American Conference on Mycorrhiza. For. Res. Lab., Corvallis, OR.

Li, C.Y., Maser, C., Maser, Z., and Caldwell, B.A. 1986. Role of three rodents in forest nitrogen fixation in western Oregon: another aspect of mammal-mycorrhizal fungus-tree mutualism. Great Basin Nat. 46:411–414.

Lovell, R. 1986. I wouldn't call forest products a declining industry. Tomorrow's forest. 1:8–11.

Lowdermilk, W.C. 1975. Conquest of the land through seven thousand years. Agricul. Inform. Bull. No. 99, U.S. Dept. of Agricul. Soil Conserv. Serv., U.S. Gov. Print. Off., Wash. D.C. 30 pp.

Macfadyen, A. 1961. Metabolism of soil invertebrates in relation to soil fertility. Ann. App. Biol. 49:215–218.

Maddock, T., III, Banks, H., DeHan, R., Harris, R., Kneese, J.H., Lehr, J.H., McCarty, P., Mercer, J., Miller, D.W., Munts, M.L., Pierle, M.A., Roisman, A.Z., Swanson, L., Tripp, J.T.B. 1984. Protecting the Nation's groundwater from contamination. Washington, D.C.: U.S. Congress, Office of Tech. Assess., OTA-0-233, 244 pp.

Margalef, R. 1969. Diversity and stability: A practical proposal and a model of interdependence. pp. 25–37. In: Diversity and stability in ecological systems. Brookhaven Symp. Biol. 22, Brookhaven Natl. Lab., Upton, NY.

Marks, G.C. and Kozlowski, T.T. 1973. Ectomycorrhizae—their ecology and physiology. Academic Press, New York, NY. 444 pp.

Maser, C. 1967. Black bear damage to Douglas-fir in Oregon. Murrelet. 48:34–38.

Maser, C. 1984. Human dignity: A diminishing resource. Outdoors West. 7:8.

Maser, C. 1985. Rangelands, wildlife technology, and human desires. pp. 83–92. In: Technologies to benefit agriculture and wildlife. Office of Tech. Assess. U.S. Congress, U.S. Gov. Print. Off., Wash., D.C.

Maser, C. 1987. Framing objectives for managing wildlife in the riparian zone on eastside federal lands. pp. 13–16. In: Managing Oregon's Riparian Zone for Timber, Fish and Wildlife. National Council of the Paper Industry for Air and Stream Improvement, Tech. Bull, No. 514.

Maser, C. 1988a. Restoration and the future of land management. J. Restor. and Manage. Notes (in press).

Maser, C. 1988b. Chief Seattle and the long view. J. Pesticide Reform 8:34–35

Maser, C., Cline, S.P., Cromack, K., Jr., Trappe, J.M., and Hansen, E. 1988b. What we know about large trees that fall to the ground. In: From the forest to the sea, a story of fallen trees. Maser, C., Tarrant, R.F.,Trappe, J.M., Franklin, J.F. (Tech. Eds.). USDA For. Serv. GTR PNW Pac. Northwest Res. Sta., Portland, OR.

Maser, C., Maser, Z., Witt, J.W., and Hunt, G. 1986. The northern flying squirrel: a mycophagist in southwestern Oregon. Can. J. Zool. 64:2086–2089.

210

Maser, C., Tarrant, R.F., Trappe, J.M., and Franklin, J.F. 1988a. From the forest to the sea, a story of fallen trees. USDA For. Serv. GTR PNW. Pac. Northwest Res. Sta., Portland, OR (in press).

Maser, C. and Trappe, J.M. (Tech. Eds.). 1984a. The seen and unseen world of the fallen tree. USDA For. Serv. Gen. Tech. Rep. PNW-164, 56 pp. Pac. Northwest For. and Range Exp. Stn., Portland, OR.

Maser, C. and Trappe, J.M. 1984b. The fallen tree—a source of diversity. pp. 335–339. In: New forests for a changing world. Proc. Soc. of Amer. For. Natl. Conf., Bethesda, MD.

Maser, C., Trappe, J.M., Li, C.Y. 1984. Large woody debris and long-term forest productivity. 6 pp. In: Proceeding Pacific Northwest Bioenergy Systems: Policies and Applications. Bonneville Power Administration, Portland, OR.

Maser, C., Trappe, J.M., and Nussbaum, R.A. 1978. Fungal-small mammal Interrelationships with emphasis on Oregon coniferous forests. Ecology 59:799–809.

Maser, Z., Maser, C., and Trappe, J.M. 1985a. Food habits of the northern flying squirrel (*Glaucomys sabrinus*) in Oregon. Can. J. Zool. 63:1084–1088.

Maser, Z., Mowrey, R., Maser, C., and Yun, W. 1985b. Northern flying squirrel: the moonlight truffler. p. 269. In: Molina, R. (Ed.). Proceedings 6th North American Conference on Mycorrhizae. For. Res. Lab., Corvallis, OR.

McCartney, S. 1986. Watering the west, part 3. Growing demand, decreasing supply send costs soaring. The Oregonian, Portland, OR. 30 September.

McKeever, S. 1960. Food of the northern flying squirrel in northeastern California. J. Mamm. 41:270–271.

Meslow, E.C., Maser, C., and Verner, J. 1981. Old-growth forests as wildlife habitat. Trans. N. Amer. Wildl. Natl Resour. Conf. 46:329–335.

Miller, O.K., Jr. 1983. Ectomycorrhizae in the Agaricales and Gastromycetes. Can. J. Bot. 61:909–916.

Monroe, B. 1986. Fees predicted in three years for hunting on federal lands. The Oregonian, Portland, OR. 3 August.

Moore, N.W., Hooper, M.D., and Davis, B.N.K. 1967. Hedges, I. Introduction and reconaissance studies. J. Appl. Ecol. 4:201–220.

Morrison, P.H. and Swanson, F.J. In press. Fire history in two forest ecosystems of the central western Cascade Range, Oregon. USDA Forest Serv. GTR, Pac. Northw. Res. Sta., Portland, OR.

211

Myers, N., Nath, U.R., and Westlake, M. 1984. Gaia, an atlas of planet management. Gaia Books Ltd., London. 272 pp.

Nelson, G. 1986. Preface. pp. i., In: conserving biological diversity in our National Forests. Norse, E.A., Rosenbaum, K.L., Wilcove, D.S., Wilcox, B.A., Romme, W.H., Johnson, D.W., Stout, M.L. Wilderness Soc., Washington, D.C.

Nierenberg, G.I. 1981. The art of negotiating. Pocket Books, New York, NY. 254 pp.

Norse, E.A., Rosenbaum, K.L., Wilcove, D.S., Wilcox, B.A., Romme, W.H., Johnson, D.W., Stout, M.L. 1986. Conserving biological diversity in our National Forests. Wilderness Soc., Wash., D.C. 116 pp.

Oort, A.J.P. 1974. Activation of spore germination in Lactarius species by volatile compounds of Ceratocystis fagacearum. Konikl. Neb. Acad. Wetensch. Ser. C. 77:301–307.

Overton, W.S. and L.M. Hunt. 1974. A view of current forest policy, with questions regarding the future state of forests and criteria of management. Trans. N. Amer. Wildl. and Nat. Resour. Conf. 39:334–353.

Patterson, L.E. and Eisenberg, S. 1983. The counseling process (3rd ed.). Houghton Mifflin Co., Boston, MA. 259 pp.

Perry, D.A. Landscape pattern and forest pests. Northw. Environ. J. (in press).

Perry, D.A. and J. Maghembe. Ecosystem concepts and current trends in forest management: Time for reappraisal. For. Ecol. and Manage. (in press).

Pessemier, E.A. 1982. Product management, strategy and organization (2nd ed.). John Wiley & Sons, Inc., New York, NY. 668 pp.

Petts, G.E. 1984. Impounded rivers, perspectives for ecological management. John Wiley & Sons Inc., New York, NY. 326 pp.

Phillips, D.R. and Van Lear, D.H. 1984. Biomass removal and nutrient drain as affected by total-tree harvest in southen pine and hardwood stands. J. For. 82:547–550.

Pimentel, D. 1971. Population control in crop systems: Monocultures and plant spatial patterns. Proceedings Tall Timbers Conference on Ecological Animal Control by Habitat Management. 2:209–220.

Pirozynski, K.A. and Malloch, D.W. 1975. The origin of land plants: a matter of mycotrophism. BioSystems. 6:153–164.

Plochmann, R. 1968. Forestry in the Federal Republic of Germany. Hill Family Foundation Series, School of Forestry, Oreg. State Univ., Corvallis. 52 pp.

Poole, D. and Williamson, L. 1983. Cut the trees and damn the recreation. Outdoor Life. 171:12, 14, 16, 21–22.

Prather, H. 1980. There is a place where you are not alone. Dolphin Book, Garden City, New York, NY. 211 pp.

Rausch, R.L. 1985. Presidential address. Parasitiology: retrospect and prospect. J. Parasitol. 71:139–151.

Robbins, W.G. 1984. Timber town, market economics in Coos Bay, Oregon, 1850 to the present. Pac. Northw. Quarterly. 75:146–155.

Robbins, W.G. 1985. The social context of forestry: the Pacific Northwest in the twentieth century. West. Hist. Quarterly. 16:413–427.

Robbins, W.G. 1988. Timber legacy: Work, culture, and community in Coos Bay, Oregon, 1850–1986. Univ. Wash. Press., Seattle, WA.

Rubner, H. 1985. Greek thought and forest science. Environ. Rev. 9:277–295.

Sachs, D. and Sollins, P. 1986. Potential effects of management practices on nitrogen nutrition and long-term productivity of western hemlock stands. For. Ecol and Manage. 17:25–36.

Sanders, S.D. 1984. Foraging by Douglas tree squirrels (ITamiasciurus douglasii: Rodentia) for conifer seeds and fungi. Ph.D. thesis, Univ. of California, Davis. 95 pp.

Schiefelbein, S. 1979. Teaching Poseidon to turn a profit. Sat. Rev., 6 January:23–25.

Schütt, P. and Cowling, E.B. 1985. Waldsterben, a general decline of forests in central Europe: symptoms, development and possible causes. Plant Disease. 69:548–558.

Senft, J.F., Bendtsen, B.A., and Galligan, W.L. 1985. Weak wood, fast-grown trees make problem lumber. J. For. 83:477–484.

Seuss, Dr. 1971. The Lorax. Random House, New York, NY. 70 pp.

Sheffield, R.M., Cost, N.D., Bechtold, W.A., McClure, J.P. 1985. Pine growth reductions in the Southeast. Resour. Bull. SE-83. U.S. For. Serv., Southeastern For. Exp. Sta. Asheville, NC. 112 pp.

Sheffield, R.M. and Cost, N.D. 1987. Behind the decline. J. For. 85:29–33.

Shigo, A.L. 1985. Wounded forests, starving trees. J. For. 83:668–673.

Shrubb, M. 1970. Birds and farming today. Bird Study. 17:123–144.

Siccama, T.G., Bliss, M., Vogelmann, H.W. 1982. Decline of red spruce in the Green Mountains of Vermont. Bull. Torrey Bot. Club. 109:163.

Sidle, R.C., Pearce, A.J., and O'Loughlin, C.L. 1985. Hillslope stability and land use. Water Resour. Monogr. Ser. 11, Amer. Geophys. Union, Wash., D.C. 140 pp.

Smuts, J.C. 1926. Holism and evolution. MacMillan and Co., Ltd, London. 361 pp.

Society of American Foresters. 1984. Acidic deposition and forests. SAF Policy Series. Bethesda, MD. 48 pp.

Soil Science Society of America. 1984. Glossary of soil science terms. Soil Sci. Soc. Amer., Madison, WI. 38 pp.

Solo, R. 1974. Problems of modern technology. J. Econ. Issues. 8:859–876.

Spies, T. and Cline, S.P. 1988. Coarse woody debris in unmanaged and managed coastal Oregon forests. In: From the forest to the sea, a story of fallen trees. Maser, C., Tarrant, R.F., Trappe, J.M. Franklin, J.F. (Tech. Eds.). USDA For. Serv. GTR PNW Pac. Northwest Res. Sta., Portland, OR (in press).

Stoessinger, J.G. 1974. Why nations go to war. St. Martin's Press, Inc., New York, NY. 230 pp.

Stoltmann, R. 1987. Hiking guide to the big trees of southwestern British Columbia. Western Canada Wilderness Committee, Vancouver, British Columbia. 144 pp.

Sullivan, M. 1986. Oregon's billion dollar bird. Tomorrow's forests. 1:12–13.

Tagliabue, J. 1986. Parts of poisoned Rhine flow lifelessly. The Oregonian, Portland, OR. 13 November.

Taylor, D.M. 1986. Nature as a mirror of changing human values. The American Theosophist 74:333–337.

Taylor, R.B. 1987. Owls or old growth? Corvallis Gazette-Times, Corvallis, OR. 8 February.

Thirgood, J.V. 1981. Man and the Mediterranean forest, a history of resource depletion. Academic Press, New York, NY. 194 pp.

Thomas, J.W. 1984. Fee-hunting on the Public Lands?—an appraisal. Trans. N. Amer. Nat. Resour. Conf. 49:455–468.

Thomas, W.L., Jr., Sauer, C.O., Bates, M., Mumford, L. (Eds.). 1956. Man's role in changing the face of the earth. Univ. Chicago Press, Chicago, IL. 1193 pp.

Trappe, J.M. 1981. Mycorrhizae and productivity of arid and semiarid rangelands. pp. 581–599. In: Advances in food producing systems or arid and semiarid lands. Academic Press, Inc., New York.

Trappe, J M. and Fogel, R.D. 1977. Ecosystematic functions of mycorrhizae. pp. 205–214. In: Marshal, J.K. (Ed.), The belowground ecosystem: a synthesis of plant-associated processes. Range Sci. Dept. Sci. Ser. 26. Colorado State Univ., Fort Collins.

Trappe, J.M. and Maser, C. 1976. Germination of spores of *Glomus macrocarpus* (Endogonaceae) after passage through a rodent digestive tract. Mycologia, 68:433–436.

Trappe, J.M. and Maser, C. 1977. Ectomycorrhizal fungi: interactions of mushrooms and truffles with beasts and trees. pp. 165–178. In: Walters, T. (Ed.), Mushrooms and man: an interdisciplinary approach to mycology. Linn Benton Comm. Coll., Albany, OR.

Trappe, J.M. and Molina, R. 1986. Taxonomy and genetics of mycorrhizal fungi: their interaction and relevance. pp. 133–146. In: Gianinazzi-Pearson, V. and Gianinazzi, S. (Eds.), Proceedings of 1st European Symposium on Mycorrhizae. Institut National Researche Agronomique, France.

U.S. Department of Agriculture, Forest Service. 1986. USDA Forest Service manual—2500-watershed. USDA For. Serv.

U.S. Laws, Statutes, etc.; Public Law 94-588. [S. 3091], Oct. 22, 1976, National Forest Management Act of 1976. pp. 2949–2963. In: United States Code Congressional and Administrative News. 94th Congr. 2d Sess., 1976. 16 U.S.C. Sec. 1600 (1976). West Publishing Co. Vol 2. St. Paul, MN.

Van Deusen, J.L. 1978. Shelterbelts on the Great Plains: What's happening? J. For. 76:160–161.

Waring, R.H. and Franklin, J.F. 1979. Evergreen coniferous forests of the Pacific Northwest. Science 204:1380–1386.

Waring, R.H. and Schlesinger, W.H. 1985. Forest ecosystems: concepts and management. Academic Press, Inc. Orlando, FL. 340 pp.

Weber, I.P. and Wiltshire, S.D. 1985. The nuclear waste primer, a handbook for citizens. The League of Women Voters Education Fund, Nick Lyons Books, New York, NY. 90 pp.

Wilkinson, C.F. 1986. Spotted owl chosen symbol of endangered old growth. The Oregonian, Portland, OR. 21 December.

Williams, W.A. 1986. Nuclear winter adds to futility of war. The Daily Barometer, Oreg. State Univ, Corvallis. 30 April.

Worster, D. 1979. Dust Bowl, the southern plains in the 1930's. Oxford Univ. Press, Inc., New York, NY. 277 pp.

Worster, D. 1985. River of empire: water, aridity, and the growth of the American west. Pantheon Books, New York, NY. 402 pp.

Wyant, D. 1986. 220-year study tracks log rot. The Register-Guard, Eugene, OR. 3 March.

Zedaker, S.M., Hyink, D.M., and Smith, D.W. 1987. Growth declines in red spruce. J. For. 85:34–36.

Zengerle, M.W. and Allan, M.A. 1987. Status reports on selected environmental issues. Volume 2: Forest decline—environmental causes. Elec. Power Res. Inst. EA-5097S-SR, Vol. 2, Res. Proj. 2662, 5002. Palo Alto, CA. pp. i–iii; 1–11; A-1–A-3; B-1–B-7.

Zhang, X.W., Guang, H., Zhen, H.Y., Hong, Y., Zhou, X.Q., Zhou, C.L. 1980. Repeated plantation of *Cunninghamia lanceolata* and toxicisis of soil. pp. 151–158. In: Ecological studies on the artificial *Cunninghamia lanceolata* forests. People's Republic of China: Inst. of For. and Soil Sci., Acad. Sinica.

# INDEX

219

221

humanity xviii, 11, 59, 65, 66, 123, 126, 163, 172, 188
humility 48, 55, 99, 102, 122, 146, 148, 169, 171, 182
Hummel 106
Hunt 151, 152
Hyatt xix

identity xix, 133, 139
Ignorance Quotient 62
imagination 44, 140, 141
inaccessible 119, 120
industry, forest 85, 92, 103, 105, 148, 151
   forest products 85
industrial 60, 103
   changes 189
   world 113
industrialist 99, 123, 163, 164, 167, 189
   argument 164
inoculate 38
insect xix, 15, 43, 53, 83, 85, 129, 170, 177
intellectual isolation 190
intuition xix
invertebrates, marine 6
   woodboring 6
Irwin 152
Italian maritime states 68
   Genoa 68
   Venice 68

Jablanczy xix
Jackman 170
Japan 52
John 137
Jones 150, 170
judgment 60, 117, 121, 123, 128, 139, 162
   economic 151
   human 162
Jung 63

Kadera 151
karma 112
Kelly 150
Kendrick 155
Kennedy 131, 165
Kimerling 154
Knight 68
knowledge, intuitive 11
   scientific 79
   rational 11–12
Kotter 36
Kozlowski 26, 29
Kubler-Ross 136
Külp 84

landscape 8, 9, 41–48, 52, 64, 91, 114, 143, 163, 179, 183
   forested 52, 128, 161
   German 76
   management 183
   of Nepal 82
   presettlement 19
larch 26, 52
Lathem 124
Leckenby 87
Lee 3
Leopold 3, 131, 157
Li 29, 31, 33, 69
lichen 25
   *Bryoria fremonti* 25
   epiphyt 25
linden 75
liquidate 93, 97, 150, 151
logic 116, 134–136, 137
Lorax 170
LORD 169, 171
Loub 71
love xviii, xix, 55, 128, 135, 136, 140, 169, 173
Lovell 85
Lowdermilk 3, 16–17

231

232

Photo by Martha Brookes

Chris Maser has spent over 20 years working as a research scientist in natural history and ecology in forest, range, subarctic, desert, and coastal setting. Trained primarily as a vertebrate zoologist, he was with the U.S. Department of the Interior Bureau of Land Management from 1975 to 1987, the last seven years spent studying the ancient forests of western Oregon. Maser authored and coauthored over 180 scientific publications before leaving the government in September 1987, and is now a private consultant in sustainable forestry. His main interests are restoration ecology and improvement of the human condition.